Come Live With Me

Come Live With Me

by

Grace Rosen Baldwin

---

with
Mary-Alice Wightman

Illustrations by
Debbie W. Woods

BRANDYLANE PUBLISHERS • Lively, Virginia 22507

Brandylane Publishers, Lively, VA 22507

© 1994 by Grace Rosen Baldwin
All rights reserved. Published 1994
Printed in the United States of America

Library of Congress Cataloging–in–Publication Data

Baldwin, Grace Rosen, 1914–
   Come live with me/ by Grace Rosen Baldwin with Mary–Alice Wightman; illustrations by Debbie W. Woods.
      p.   cm.
   ISBN 1-883911-02-8: $14.95
   1. Baldwin, Grace Rosen, 1914–   . 2. Women benefactors—Virginia—Richmond—Biography. 3. Women—Housing—Virginia—Richmond—History—20th century. 4. Lodging–houses—Virginia—Richmond—History—20th century. I. Wightman, Mary–Alice, 1927–   II. Title.
HD7288.6.U6B35 1994
363.5 ' 574 ' 092—dc20
[B]   94–29930
                                                               CIP

Dedicated to

"All The Girls"

and my family: my husband, Everette S. Baldwin, Sr.; my son and his family, Charles Hunter Jones, Ardenia Jones, Deena J. Kane, William R. Kane, Kristin Kane; my siblings, Howard L. Rosen, Jesse F. Rosen, Frances Kirby, Virginia Butler, Addie Vaughn and Phyllis Clark.

Life, what a beautiful dream when it becomes true. It is a life of love, joy and excitement because over a thousand of you played true characters on my stages of life.

My long life is full of golden memories as I celebrate my 80th birthday, remembering the days you came and lived with me.

Love,

Grace Rosen Baldwin
1994 Richmond, Virginia

CHAPTER I

The theme of life for me would be
Four profound words, "Come live with me."

In the very early years of the twentieth century I was a young girl with a special daydream. It had no name then, but the dream continued through the years to play in my mind as a little girl and prevailed as I grew into womanhood. My childhood, sheltered within a loving family, was most pleasant. I knew many happy times growing up on a typical farm in rural Buckingham County, Virginia. My home was almost centered between the Blue Ridge Mountains some forty miles in the west and the capital city, Richmond, sixty miles to the east. The beautiful blue that gave the ancient rounded mountains their name was visible in the distance, but the city, like the dream it held, was not within sight from that area. With the added joy of visiting often on my grandfather's farm, a short eight miles from my home, I always felt loved and secure at both places. There was no need for a dream then.

I was Grace Clark Rosen, middle child of Bessie Crews and Henry Rosen, born September 9, 1914. My sister, Frances, had her birthday on September 5, and like many things we shared, our close birthdays were celebrated on the 7th. We also shared an older brother, Robert, and two younger sisters, Virginia and Mabel. Lined up by ages, from two to ten, the Rosen children stood like stairsteps. I was not one to stand still for long though, and I soon matched my sister in size.

Listening to my mother teach Frances the first year of schooling at home, I was quick to learn. My mother had put aside her nursing profession to raise her children. She instilled in all of us her own belief and faith in God, and she taught us to pray at an early age. Using the skill inherited from her own mother, a fine tailoress, my mother made our clothes. The plain little dresses were just right for me. In one of these I proudly began

first grade on my sixth birthday at Buckingham School. Three classes were taught in the same room, and I could hardly wait to give the right answers, even those asked the higher grades. I would wave my hand and sometimes blurt out the answer even when Frances, knowing the answer, sat quietly. The teacher finally punished me, making me write on the blackboard, "I must not talk," one hundred times. My short fingers were numb before I finished.

In that year of young innocence, I had a best friend, and my mother made both of us identical dresses in different colors with matching pants. One was blue gingham, and the other, red gingham. When we went down to the bathrooms in the basement of the school, an older student took advantage of our short legs dangling from the high seats, grabbed our colorful pants, and ran out. She slipped both pairs over a stick and marched around the hall singing, "Three cheers for the red, white and blue." We came running back, crying for our pants, and the boys kept asking us, "You don't have your pants? Let's see!" Dutifully we would bend over to show them. This was repeated several times amid much laughter before the teacher came and put an end to the childish prank.

Henry Rosen, my father, had two farms, raising crops, cattle, horses, pigs, and chickens quite successfully. Food was abundant, my mother was a wonderful cook, and I was always hungry. Like all the children, I had jobs to help with the farming even when I was quite little, and even at grandfather's farm. During a very deep snow when I was visiting there, grandfather shoveled a path to the barn. It was almost like a tunnel, and when grandmother sent me on an errand to the barn, she could not even see the top of my woolen stocking cap above the tunnel. She would make me carry a broomstick with a bright rag tied on the end. Then as long as the flag was waving, grandmother knew all was well.

All of us children loved the farms where we made our own fun after our chores were done, growing together in love and harmony. Taking the buggy for a visit to our grandparents' farm was an exciting adventure. Along the way we often stopped at a maple tree where Robert would chop a plug out of the trunk of the tree and hang a can underneath the opening to catch the syrup. Then we would wait to have a taste. It was good and sweet to my sisters and me, but sometimes it was as hard as chewing gum.

On one of our visits to grandfather's farm, Robert and I climbed into the loft of the barn and found three large cream-colored eggs with brown markings. We only took two, one for each of us, and boiled the eggs in a tin can over the outside fire where our grandmother heated water in a large black kettle for washing clothes. Playing camping, we ate the hardboiled eggs and thought they were delicious. On our next visit Robert and I returned to the barn and discovered the third egg had hatched into a small white bird. It was a baby turkey buzzard!

Laughter and peacefulness dominated life on the farms during those wonderful young years. My early love of all that is beautiful encompassed our big garden and the fragrant orchards of fruit trees in blossom which yielded cherries, apples, plums, and peaches. I was delighted with the spring of cool pure water where mint grew as high as the top of my reddish-blond curls. I played under shady trees during the hot summers amid the fragrance of flowers which my mother tended, and I watched the leaves turning colors as the seasons changed. I was unaware of the war which raged in the world at that time, or that my life would change, too. There was a quiet strength growing within me that would carry me through many changes.

In my childhood the spunkiness within me made me tactlessly outspoken whenever I was made to feel less than equal to another person. One of those times was after peace had returned to the world with the armistice of November 1918. The following summer Uncle Harvey was returning from his service in Europe. Harvey was a cousin of mine, but he was Uncle Harvey to my cousin, Bea. The family was very proud because he had received distinguished honors as an army captain in World War I. Grandmother had prepared a room for him at her home, and reminded those helping her, "Be sure and sterilize all of Harvey's clothes when he comes because he might have lice or itch."

Because I was visiting her at the time, Granny took me to the train station to welcome Harvey, and everyone was wild with excitement over this hero. There was a crowd waiting for him, and I wanted to see, too. Bea pushed me behind the crowd, saying, "He is not your Uncle Harvey. You can't call him that."

Seething within at being dwarfed behind the others, it all boiled over when I did meet Harvey. "I am glad you are not my uncle 'cause you have all those lice and itch." Grandmother pulled me aside as quickly as she could, but I did not understand why at the time.

The summer of 1921, in the fullness of a joy that matched the peacefulness of the world and our land, my family moved into our new farmhouse. Though as yet unfinished, this larger home had running water and a windmill to generate electricity, luxuries we had not known before. Scaffolding was still attached to the house for the last coat of paint to be applied. The porch ceiling would be completed after the double swing was hung, and much lumber was piled high in the front yard. It was a hot August day. Without warning tragedy shocked our family like a cold black ocean wave splashing over us. All the sunshine and lightheartedness vanished. My mother had suffered a miscarriage, and complications took her life suddenly. Her last words, "Take care of my little children," rang out like a death peal. With so much to live for and so much love to give, our mother was taken from us.

Devastated after the funeral and deeply sorrowful, my father climbed up on the lumber, slumped down and buried his head in his strong hands. His other little ones did not fully understand, nor did I, but in our desire to comfort him, we too climbed up on the pile of lumber and sat in a circle around our daddy. He spoke not one word. As all five of us huddled close against him, even our love could not console the loss of his dear Bessie. To raise five children alone, four of them such little girls, was a task beyond him in his grief.

Time heals, but for awhile time stood still for our grieving

Come Live With Me

family there on the lumber pile. As the sun began to set, I began to feel hungry. It was time to eat, but I knew my daddy had never cooked anything in his life. Grandmother knew this, and she knew some decisions had to be made. A shrewd, intelligent woman, she marched over to the lumber pile in full command, looked up and said, "Henry, you cannot take care of these children, and we don't want them put in an orphanage. I am going to ask the family to take the children so they can get together sometimes and see each other in case of sickness."

With the abruptness and finality of this decision began the realization for me and the children that our loss was permanent. Within my own young heart, I knew our happy family would never be together again. Other family members gathered around and began talking to all of the children, as we sat on the lumber pile with our daddy. Watching from my perch atop the lumber, I heard Aunt Sadie say, "Come live with me," as she took Mabel who was still in diapers. I listened as Virginia went along with another aunt. Soon my whole family would be completely scattered, Robert being the only one left with my daddy. I longed to hear "come live with me" from Aunt Mamie who looked the most like my mother, and whose husband I liked a great deal. Uncle Bernard and I had become good buddies the summer before when he was courting my aunt. Now a young bride, Mamie was talking of nothing except her honeymoon. There was no thought on that day of having a child living with her.

Since all of my aunts were quite young, the grandparents had decided that the great aunts were much more qualified to raise the children. It was Aunt Laura who came to me and said, "Come live with me."

To my little six-year-old mind, this great aunt seemed very old. She was at least forty! I wondered how long it had been since Aunt Laura had a little girl live with her. Yet, "Come live with me" filled me with a tingling excitement. I was going to live with my rich aunt in Richmond! There the beginning of my daydream awaited me.

CHAPTER II

*A dream came to me silently,
A house that said, "Come live with me."*

Having always lived in the country within the warmth and security of my family, suddenly moving to a big city sixty miles away from all I had ever known, proved frightening, lonely, and at the same time exciting. The very first day in my new home in Richmond, I was taken downtown by Aunt Laura and a maid to a fine department store. Never had such a fuss been made over me. The salesladies helped me up on the counter and tried a variety of pretty dresses on me. There were blue, pink, yellow, and red creations with shoes and socks to match. Of course, I had never been in a store like that because my clothes had been made at home. This was such fun! I would turn around and whirl the full skirts above my knees to show the matching pants which came with each fancy dress. I was fitted for patent leather shoes and a pair of t-strap sandals I chose myself. I was a farmer's daughter, but I felt like a princess ready for a ball in a beautiful castle!

The "ball" was my next excitement. It was a special party given for me and Aunt Laura and Uncle Phil, to celebrate and officially claim me as their new daughter. The host and hostess lived on Monument Avenue, the most fashionable area of the city. The house, an elaborate three-story residence of brick and

Come Live With Me

stone masonry, had been built for the owner's bride about the same year that I was born. Its design of Tudor and Gothic features with lovely pointed archways across the entrance gave it the appearance of a small castle.

The lights in the castle shone from its many windows like stars in a magic sky. I gazed in wonder and felt the magic. I was awestruck as I entered the spacious foyer. Here we were graciously welcomed amid the greetings of friends in long formal evening gowns. Music floated from the adjoining living room where young ladies and men were dancing. The floor-length windows on either side of the fireplace opened as doors, leading out to the open porch which extended around from the covered entrance at the front door.

Behind the living room was a library, one side lined with shelves of books, and the opposite wall had a cushioned window seat in a huge bay window which faced the side garden. This dark-paneled room also opened into the far end of the entrance foyer and directly across from the lovely staircase on which couples mingled, some of them laughing and kissing. Beyond this area of the foyer was the dining room in which a long buffet table was spread with an inviting feast of food. The tinkling of glasses blended with the dance music and the laughter of the celebrating crowd. They had come to celebrate with me, but there were no other children, not even one, at the party for me.

In spite of my loneliness I stood when asked, reciting poems, singing songs, and performing like a seal. I knew so many rhymes my mother had taught me, and I tried to speak them clearly with expression to match the grandeur of my frilly party dress. The guests showered me with compliments as they gathered around me for a short while, but when the entertainment was over I wandered back into the foyer. Feeling so homesick for my own family that I wanted to disappear, I headed alone toward a big platform rocker covered in red velvet. The legs had brass feet on the bottom that looked like lion claws. I carefully avoided these as I climbed into the soft-stuffed chair. From my comfortable hideaway, I looked at the beautiful dark, wooden carving of the stairway rising above a glittering chandelier. The prisms of the lights shown like sunshine on a frozen field of snow. As I watched the shadows from the dancing figures play across the sparkling lights, my loneliness gave way to sleepiness. My heart was as heavy as my eyes began to feel. How I longed for another little girl to be with me.

"Someday I'll buy this house and have all the little seven-year-old girls in the world come live with me." This ambitious thought came to me without seeming like an impossible dream. I had heard my aunts often say that Bessie's children would inherit some money later on. Not being too anxious to get down from the chair since I would have to pass those scary legs, I snuggled deeper into the red velvet. I fell asleep dreaming of my house with all the girls.

The clapping of hands and the laughter in the adjoining room awakened me. Everyone had stopped dancing and was telling the butler how great he had done his job. Wearing a white jacket and dark trousers and carrying a towel over his arm, he had answered every beck and call all evening. There was a pedal on the floor in the dining room to summon the servant, like in many of the large houses at that time. It made a clanking sound, and whenever it was heard this butler would come with a dish or bottle. He was pleased with the appreciation shown by the guests for his service. Tall, strong, and courteous, the black man was smiling when he came over to help me out of the chair. Right away I looked up at him towering above my tiny frame and said, "You can keep your job when I grow up and buy this house because I like you too."

All of the girls and boys of the families who had lived next to our farm had been my friends. The black children were included in the annual Easter egg hunts at grandmother's, and we had many good times together during all the seasons. Suddenly I missed those friends too.

Later that night back in my lovely new bed with a maid tucking me in, I longed for the days with my brother and sisters at our home in the country. In my homesick heart the miles

Come Live With Me

between us seemed to stretch around the world. I squeezed my eyes tight to keep the maid from seeing my tears. Silently I went through the members of my family, calling each name, asking God to bless them. This brought me a comfort much like the presence of my mother who had taught me that God was always there with me. Somehow the party seemed more like a dream to me, but my daydream was very real. I truly wanted that house "when I got my money," where I could have lots of little girls my age come live with me. The intensity of my longing continued through the years with a faith that never faltered.

CHAPTER III

*Known as the "arithmetic girl,"
The one "left over" in the world.*

Aunt Laura's house was spacious and elegant. The furnishings were gorgeous, but everything was so entirely different for me. Though it offered every material comfort, my new home was a miserably unhappy place for me. I was such a lonely little girl. Even the canary, parrot, and bulldog were strange to me. Never seeming to adjust, I did make friends with the dog, Jep. One day I went out to play with him. There was a high wooden fence surrounding the well-kept yard, and I wandered around until I noticed a tree full of peaches. I climbed up quickly and shook the branches. Of course only the wormy peaches fell, but that was okay. I was smart enough to pick the good part out, and Jep liked the rest. Sitting under the tree, I enjoyed all the peaches within reach. Jep remained near me, waiting for his next bite, and that made me feel less lonely. My spanking clean clothes were pretty full of peaches when Aunt Laura came running out of the house.

"Look at you! Oh, poor Bessie's children. This child will never adjust!" She grabbed me, rushed in the house, gave me a bath, and dressed me fresh again. Then she placed a large white barber's apron over the front of me to protect my pretty dress and tied it at the back of my neck. Aunt Laura sat me in a chair at the dining room table. The maid had been sent to the store, and she soon returned with the largest, most beautiful peaches I had ever seen. The lovely peaches were carefully peeled and put in a crystal dish which was placed on a silver plate with a doily under that. Then the maid spooned whipped cream over the peaches and added a big red cherry on top. The scrumptious treat was placed in front of me, but I had already eaten almost half a bushel of wormy peaches, fuzz and all. I did not want any more peaches!

Pointing her finger at me, Aunt Laura said, "Eat all of

them." She went into the next room, and I got mad.

I got real mad, partly because I was all spotlessly clean and partly because I missed my family more than ever. I sat there pouting. Looking across the room at the sideboard where many bottles and decanters were lined up neatly, I remembered how Uncle Phil acted whenever he got mad. He would get up from the table while my aunt kept talking and talking, and walk over to the sideboard and pour a glass of sherry. Uncle Phil would say, "To heck with it," throw his head back, drain the glass, set it down with a thud, and walk out without eating. That was the only time Aunt Laura did not say another word for a long while.

This started me thinking, "I'll try that." I slipped down from the chair, walked over in front of the array of bottles and read "SHERRY" on one fancy decanter. Unable to reach that high, I pushed a chair to the sideboard, climbed up, and poured a large glass like Uncle Phil had done. In one swift motion I gulped it down. As I set the glass down easily, Aunt Laura called from the other room.

"Have you eaten your peaches? If you don't, I will punish you."

Jumping down from the chair, I started back to the table. Everything started turning around, then the ceiling began whirling in circles, and I couldn't stand up. I sat down on the floor. The table was rolling around toward me, and I rolled underneath it, moaning in agony. As I rolled around the big apron covered my head. When my aunt found me lying there crying and the peaches uneaten, she ran out screaming. Aunt Laura had never had children, and she did not know what to do with me, sick, and white as the apron. She called Aunt Mamie.

"Come and get Grace. She is ill."

Within the hour Uncle Bernard arrived from Rockville where he and Mamie were living. He brought me back through Hanover County to see a doctor in the town of Ashland. Here the Randolph Macon College campus bordered the main street in the center of town, and the railroad went straight down the middle of the street. I could hear the train chugging by as the doctor pumped out my stomach. The peaches and sherry had turned to brandy, and the doctor asked, "What have you been eating?"

"I just had a glass of 'to heck with it' like Uncle Phil, but he never laid on the floor crying with the pain from it."

Soon recovered and living with Aunt Mamie as I had longed to do, I attended Armstrong School in Rockville. Each morning Professor Cox would stop by for me in his two-wheel jumper pulled by a spirited horse. I had to hold on tight with both hands to keep from being bounced right off the seat, but I was happy.

Happy, that is, until plans were made for me to live with Aunt Lottie who was really an older cousin in Buckingham. After Christmas Aunt Mamie and I went back to grandmother's house and stayed while arrangements were completed for this move. Frances was living there with our grandmother at the time. Everyone kept saying how wonderful that I would have this advantage, but I rebelled.

"If it is so great, then let my sister, Frances, have the golden opportunity."

Grandmother looked at me in surprise. "Okay, but whoever goes gets all the pretty new clothes that were bought for you, Grace. They will fit Frances too, you know."

I knew that, and it was all right with me. I had already seen my grandmother sewing some beautiful clothes and putting them in the trunk in the parlor. One day the key was left in the trunk, and I sneaked in, opened the trunk, and held the clothes up to me. The little dresses came right to my knees, and I liked them! So I talked my sister into going to live with Aunt Lottie, and Frances grew up there very well cared for while I continued to search for my own special place in life.

Staying on at grandmother's, I wondered how long it would be before they would feel sorry and bring out the trunk of clothes for me. It was the day the doctor came and everybody was in a hustle and bustle that I learned the answer. They locked me outside, and when I peeped in the parlor window I saw the trunk being carried to the bedroom where Aunt Mamie was staying. It wasn't long before I heard a baby crying in that bedroom. My high hopes were dashed again. Aunt Mamie would not have time for me now. Those clothes were for Mamie's new baby! The dresses had looked long enough, but like me, they did not fit.

Through the years I continued to be sent from one place to another and was described as the "arithmetic girl," meaning the one left over. I became adaptable to change, moving from one house and family to the next, and from one school to another. No one realized the turmoil within me, nor could I understand it myself. It remained a vague restlessness, a desire to belong and to matter. I did not fully understand, but simply kept striving to be something more to others. Perhaps that was why I so willingly packed up and went whenever someone in the family called for me to come live with them. Wherever needed, I was capable of being a great help in all household tasks and especially whenever a baby was born in a family. Even before my teen years I would take the newborn in my arms and bathe the baby. I felt no fear with this awesome responsibility. No matter what, the arithmetic girl was considered dependable. Those who knew me best would remark, "All you have to do is praise Grace, and she will do anything that needs doing."

Some of the best times for me were spent in Manteo, an area near Buckingham Courthouse, with my mother's brother, Uncle Harry, and his wife, Aunt Bessie. I always felt at home there. They had five fine sons and a lovely daughter, Christine. These cousins became dear friends, especially Christine, as we were almost the same age. It was wonderful being a part of this happy family.

Henry Rosen wanted to have his children together again as a family too, and after his second marriage he asked the girls to come home. I was filled with excitement at this prospect, but my imagination dealt me a blow. In my longing for my mother, somehow I expected my new mother would be just like Bessie—tall, dark haired, with deep brown eyes that shone with her tender love.

On the day my sisters and I returned home, our stepmother's sister was also there. I saw the full, short figure of a young blond lady with blue eyes and knew that could not be my mother. I ran to hug the dark haired lady who was more like the mother I remembered. Naturally my stepmother, Mary, was eager to have Henry's girls accept her and felt upset by this. It was awkward for all of us at first, but I grew to love my stepmother. Mary was a very caring person and good to all of us, but she had a task not easy for one so young. She simply did not always have the time each of us longed for with her, and even less as she began her own family of six children.

Come Live With Me

Frances remained with Aunt Lottie, but the rest of us settled in with our daddy and Mary. I continued on my merry-go-round, moving whenever another family needed me. Even changing schools so often, I remained a good student and sang in the choirs at school and church which I attended regularly. Yet I never forgot my old daydream longing to have "all the girls my age in the world live with me."

It was my brother, Robert, who found a handwritten deed in an old trunk to the land our mother, Bessie, had bought on August 14, 1914. That date was the month before I was born, and the deed was in Bessie's name. With it was a paper written by her stating, "This is for my unborn son, Jessie Clark Rosen." When Robert showed this to me, I was puzzled and questioned my daddy.

"Why was my name that way?"

Daddy looked at me. "Bessie was so positive you were a boy, she called you Jessie in honor of her father. You see, Gracie, right before you were born, we had hurriedly built a corn house with an attached one-hole johnny house on that land where we planned to build our home. We sent your brother and sister to stay with their grandparents until we had a larger house. We were living in that little house when you arrived, a pug-nosed baby girl, kicking and screaming. It was four o'clock in the morning, and at that early hour the only light in the room was a kerosene lantern hanging from a nail."

A smile came over my daddy's face as he continued explaining to me. "Bessie took one look at you and said, 'Oh, Lord, give me grace!' The midwife handed you to me, and I named you Gracie Clarkie after my aunt. In the darkness of that early September morning spelling mistakes were made. Your mother corrected that in 1920 when she registered all of you, our five children. She wrote your name 'Gracie Clark'."

Daddy's story reassured me that my mother had loved me and all of her children very much. I still missed my mother, especially when Robert teased me. Often he would chant, "Gracie Clarkie, Gracie Clarkie!" Those were fighting words that made me mad. Robert would soon make up—whenever he wanted me to fill a left-over place in his playing or working. Yet his teasing was partially responsible for me having my name legally changed later to "Grace Clark."

The most difficult part of being the arithmetic girl was not having any space left over for me. Even with my daddy and Mary, I never had a closet for my things or one to share. My clothes had to hang on a hook behind the door of the bedroom I shared. During one of the times at home I was asked to sing at the funeral of Uncle Zach who had lived behind our farm. This older black man had worked on the farm for years and was highly respected.

The morning of the funeral I started out to the farm where he had lived. Along the way I came upon a long roomy box made of smooth wood. One look and I imagined it standing on end with the lid a door. Here was a perfect closet! Hurriedly I dragged the box through a field of broomstraw, a shortcut back to the house. Pulling it into my room, I left it in a corner and rushed back to the funeral. An organ which had been placed outside for the service was playing, and when the strains of "He Leadeth Me" began, I proudly stood and sang all the words of the hymn. The preacher delivered his funeral oratory, and in his closing prayer he raised his voice to a loud pitch. "God have mercy on the soul that stole the box."

I ran over to my daddy. "I have the box!" He calmly sent for another box used to protect the coffin at the gravesite and paid $13.63 to cover the cost. The road into the cemetery had been so muddy, the funeral director had left the box along the road when he returned for a wagon needed to get through. I did get to keep my stolen closet which I nailed to the wall and enjoyed, attaching an old broomstick inside for the clothes rod. It was worth every penny I had to repay although my fingers were stained that summer from picking berries, peas, and hoeing corn to make enough money. Daddy kept a written record each time I made a payment, sometimes only 5¢, until my debt was paid in full.

As I struggled to clear this debt, the struggles within me, the arithmetic girl, grew. I was now daydreaming of having all the twelve-year-old girls in the world come live with me.

CHAPTER IV

*And then I understood in part,
The deep love in my father's heart.*

I had much growing up ahead, and having an older brother often got me in trouble. One morning Robert and I were sent down near the road to mind the cows that were being allowed to graze there without a fence. I ran about picking buttercups to make a golden necklace. Then I sat down beside Robert, who was sprawled on the grass. We were watching the fluffy clouds for animal shapes when an advertising agent came by. He asked could he put up a canvas advertising chewing tobacco on the brick shed by the road. That shed did not belong to our daddy, but Robert, thinking of the canvas as a wonderful tent for us, took charge and said, "Yes, sir."

Watching the painted canvas being attached to the building with ropes, Robert decided two canvasses would make a much better tent. He then suggested the agent put his ad on both sides of the shed. This kept the man working into the afternoon, and it was one hot day. I was hot too. When the job was finished the agent offered Robert a sample package of miniature plugs of the chewing tobacco, saying, "Give these to your daddy."

Robert, scheming again, asked, "What about her daddy?" I was given two miniature plugs of chewing tobacco, and the worker went on his way. Watching Robert as he began chewing the end of a plug from the package, I copied "big brother."

"I can't wait to tell Daddy about all this," I mumbled as I chewed.

Robert jumped up and slapped me across the back, and I swallowed the whole miniature plug. By the time we reached the house, I was black, blue, and green all over. Our stepmother took one look at me and said, "You poor dear!" Right away she hitched up the horse and buggy to take me to the doctor, not knowing what had made me ill. Robert was sent to get Daddy out of the field, and he told him what had made me sick. When I saw the look on my daddy's face, I ran under the rose arbor to avoid a whipping. Lying there as limp as the wilted buttercups that drooped around my neck, I vowed, "I will never chew or smoke tobacco, never again."

The turbulent twelves became a turning-around time for me in my thinking and attitude. Called back often to help with Daddy's second family as it grew rapidly, I began to resent the work which fell on my shoulders in the care of the younger children. I dearly loved all of my half sisters and brothers. Each one, Willie, Beatrice, Howard, Addie, Jesse, and Phyllis, were very dear to me. My heart ached because I felt no one had time for me. I transferred my own hurt, unknowingly, to a sullen disposition. Everyone was expected to help in the building of a larger house for this growing family. The days grew hotter as I carried rocks across the field for the basement of the new house. Weary from the heavy loads with little appreciation shown to me, I grew angry and resentful. Before the day was over I had decided the best solution was to run away, and I quietly disappeared.

The only plan I had was to get to my grandparents' farm. I headed through the woods before sunset and walked all night, sitting down occasionally and resting against a tree. In the darkness I wandered in circles until the early morning. At daybreak I came into a meadow and could see lights in the barn at some distance. I picked a blade of grass and blew it like a whistle. This had long been the special communication Grandfather and I had as our secret signal. He recognized the sound and answered back. Soon he was across the meadow on his horse and took me, riding double, to the house. Grandmother fed and bathed me and let me go to bed. I begged both of them not to tell my daddy, but they said they would have to tell the truth if he came looking for me. Of course, the family had missed me the night before, but Daddy felt sure where I had gone. I was weary and had been asleep only an hour, when Daddy rode over on my horse, Julie. "I want Grace to come home."

He waited for my grandmother to wake me, and he climbed back up on Julie as I came outside, tired and sleepy. "Am I going to ride in the front or back?"

"How did you get here?" That was all Daddy said so I began the walk home. After about two miles I said to myself, "I have had enough. I'm not taking this anymore." I ran over to a ditch and laid down. Daddy got off the horse to get a switch because he was not taking anymore! Then I yelled, "Go home, Julie." I knew my horse would obey me.

Daddy yelled louder, "Whoa, Julie!" Julie stood still.

Quickly I was on my feet and commanded, "Whoa, Julie, go home." Julie went home, leaving Daddy and me to walk home together.

We walked in silence a little while. Then Daddy asked me, "Why did you run away?"

"I'm tired of being a slave for the family and working and there is no end and nothing for me." The words poured out from my bottled-up heart. "My stepmother doesn't have time for me 'cause she has so many children of her own. She is too busy, and I don't think you want me either!"

Daddy walked along quietly for a short distance. "You know, Gracie, your mother didn't leave us by choice. God took her away. She was my first love, and I will always love you children, but it is my duty now to care for this family. I love them too. That doesn't make me love you any less."

For awhile only the soft sound of our footsteps broke the silence in the woods. "Your mother and I loved you and all of our children so much. We were a team working together for the same goals. We wanted each of you to have a good education, but most of all we wanted you to know God and be aware of the many gifts from God. You have talents to be proud of, and we wanted you to grow up and use them for the glory of God."

As we walked along talking together, I began to understand my daddy as never before. I felt closer to him with a stronger love than I had ever known. Daddy took my hand as we neared the house, and I looked up and saw the deep love for me in his eyes. It was a turning point for me, the little daydreamer. I still wanted a place of my own and was determined to find it, but I felt kinder towards others. The gratitude that filled my heart pushed out the resentment I had harbored.

Returning home that morning, I had a warmer feeling of love than I had known since my mother died. The words of those favorite hymns which I sang so joyfully each Sunday called out to me in a compelling way. It was not long before I knew I wanted to follow Jesus and make my life more meaningful for Him. His forgiving love had freed me to forgive too. What a beautiful Sunday when I was baptized in the creek near Maysville Baptist Church with my brother and sister! Whatever plan God had for me, I was ready and waiting.

CHAPTER V

My first fine goal would disappear,
And one, more golden, would appear.

Life revolved for me from house to house which kept me moving to different schools and even another church. Mulberry Grove Baptist Church greatly influenced my longing to become a nurse. This ambition continued as the calls from families came whenever there was sickness or another baby due. I loved the families and friends who counted on my willing help and called, "Come live with me."

When twin boys arrived at the home of my daddy's cousin, I was there. The father-to-be was extremely excited. Nervously waiting for the babies to be born, he planted two good-sized trees in his yard to shade the house. When the first baby boy was born, the new father ran out in the yard and pulled up one of the trees. This made no sense, but feeling powerless, he had to do something, anything! He returned, pacing the floor until the next little boy was born. The new father ran back out and pulled the other tree up! I cautioned him too late, "Don't do that to your property."

He was overcome beyond reason. "I can get more trees, but I have to get names for my boys."

The doctor suggested one son be named Sam, and the father named his other son, Doc. I replanted the two trees to grow in honor of Sam and Doc. Growing within me was a strong desire for the nursing profession which my mother had followed.

It was Aunt Lou, our black neighbor, who taught me many skills in cooking and sewing. Her kind words were encouraging to me, the arithmetic girl. Her praise was sincere. "You are going to amount to something. You are so quick to learn. Keep it up, and always be fair."

In that spirit with my new goal ahead, I kept my grades high. After attending eleven different schools, I was to graduate from

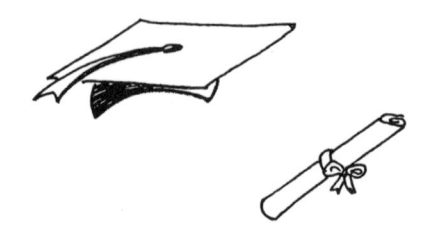

Buckingham High, the same school building where I began first grade. In that senior year I was living with Aunt Bessie when I had appendicitis and surgery was required. Much care was taken, remembering the tragic death of my baby sister, Mabel, who was only nine years old when she failed to recover from appendicitis. During the two months convalescence at Aunt Bessie's home, I studied and kept up my assignments and excellent records.

It was a proud time for me, reaching the highest grade average in the class, although I did not qualify to have my name engraved on the gold plaque that hung in the school. The longstanding rules required a student to have attended four years at the school to have this distinction, but this did not lessen the accomplishment for me.

After graduation, I felt the love and pride of my grandfather when he paid my tuition to begin nurse's training. I was soon off to Charlottesville and adjusted to this move beautifully. This was a happy time, and I did so well in the first few weeks of training that I won the "Miss Health" contest. It was a wonderful honor with my picture in the newspapers for all to see! Things were finally looking up for me, but the publicity brought attention to me and to my age. I was not yet eighteen as required for a student nurse, and the rules had to be followed. My broken dreams followed me home and hung over me like a black cloud. I had not known what people meant by the depression in the world at that time. In my own depression that winter I learned the hard cold facts. Jobs were not available. What could I do now? The question nagged and depressed me in my confusion. I felt so mixed up inside. Having to come back home with my nursing hopes dashed brought my spirits to their lowest ebb. Somehow I did not feel I belonged anywhere. The tides of disappointment had swept away the very comfort I could have leaned on. I had forgotten to pray. I had forgotten the Friend I had promised to follow, and I struggled alone.

Slowly my faith and my old dream returned. "When I get my money I am going to buy a house for all the girls my age to come live with me. Surely this is the worst age for a girl to be alone." Longing to be useful and to feel like an important part of a family, I found volunteer work at the Methodist Orphanage on West Broad Street in Richmond. This was officially known as the Virginia Annual Conference Orphanage during those years.

The next few months living and working there were the prelude before I met someone else who was lonely. He was a restless, happy-go-lucky type who had worked for the funeral director and remembered the box that disappeared. Our shared laughter was the main tie between us, but we were young and happy enough to think it was good enough for marriage. After a brief courtship, we were married that summer. Neither one of us was aware nor ready for the heavy responsibilities which would follow. The next summer our son, Charles, was born. I glowed with the happiness of motherhood, but my marriage began to crumble. Charles was still a little boy when I was left to raise him alone.

Only the many joyous hours of love and caring for this dear son, whom I would cherish forever, overshadowed the tough times working to support him. Now my goal in life became a really golden one—this family of my own. The next few years were not easy, but they were most precious as Charles and I began growing up together. I grew closer to God again and guided my son in the foundation of a Christian life.

CHAPTER VI

*A new beginning, a new love,
Surely sent me from God above.*

Happiness for me was seeing Charles take his first little steps and watching his progress. Like the years that swiftly followed, one after the other, he walked and ran and skipped. Learning to read, he was in school when the force of World War II invaded the peace of our homeland. I yearned to serve my country as a nurse, and I went down to the recruiting station in Richmond to enlist in the WACS. Both the Army and the Navy said, "No" because my son was under twelve years of age and I was his sole guardian. They could not take me unless I gave up my parental rights, and I could never do that. Charles was all I had, and he meant everything to me.

Before I returned to Buckingham a friend arranged a blind date for me. Everette Baldwin stood tall and strong when we met. His youthful good looks hid the eighteen years difference in our ages. His eyes were sincere and his manner was kind and gentle. Yet I was not very impressed at the time. He talked about his three little boys and I told him of my son. My heart was simply blind to his sterling qualities, and we both went our separate ways.

Several years later I returned to Richmond, arranging to rent a house on Floyd Avenue that I hoped eventually to purchase. Spurred by my old dream, I planned to have girls room there. In the bright morning sunshine, I walked by the stores on Broad Street, passing several window shoppers staring into the store windows. One of them saw my reflection in the shiny glass as I passed by and recognized me immediately. He rushed over and touched my arm. I turned quickly to face Everette Baldwin looking at me intently. "I have been looking for you since that first date. Please don't leave again. I love you, Grace. I want you to be my wife and come live with me."

Those four little words from my dream were like a sudden spark. I looked at Everette and knew this was the love I had been looking for. There was no explanation, only a sure feeling that God had sent me back to meet him again. My heart overflowed with happiness and love. Our marriage would be the fulfillment of my daydream of all the years. I would have a house, only it would be "all the boys" coming to live with me! Such elation filled me that I wondered why I had ever dreamed of "all the girls."

Later I learned that was not all. A whole family was coming to live with us. It was the family that had helped Everette with the arduous task of raising his sons alone. The mother had watched out for Everette's boys while he worked, and he felt an obligation to them. I understood because I remembered my own daddy unable to care for his little ones alone. Now this family was looking for a place to live too. Of course, I said, "Come live with me."

By December the house on Floyd Avenue was ready for all of us, and Everette and I were married there by a Baptist minister. He prayed that our love be like the perfect circle of my golden wedding band—forever without ending. As I stood in my bridal suit of magenta with a lovely white corsage, Everette looked at me and he repeated over and over, "Until death do us part." I felt an overwhelming love and protection from Everette as he looked into my eyes, repeating those words like a promise of faithfulness. This was the beginning of our marriage, the start of a journey we would walk together in love and faith.

Our boys settled in nicely. All four were like brothers and close in age with Robert–fourteen, Bernard–twelve, Charles–now eleven, and Claude–ten years and four months, making the three youngest almost like triplets. I was very proud of my new family, and my days were filled with the care of them. We had divided the house equally so we had the first floor rooms, and the other family lived upstairs. There were only four of them up there at first, the husband, wife, her father, and a daughter, plus the two dogs and a bantam hen. The dogs were so smart they knew how to get food from the step-on garbage can and close the lid. The hen was a creature of habit. From her perch on the upstairs railing she deposited one egg daily on the window sill below as Everette and I ate breakfast. This habit became a messy nuisance, but we laughed about it each morning before Everette went off to work.

Everette enjoyed working as a builder and had become superintendent of Doyle & Russel Construction Company. In this capacity he had many men working under his supervision. One of them was a big lazy individual who was not pulling his load. Everette was almost forced to fire him, but disliking that idea, he looked for some other potential in the man. When he called this employee in, he offered him a raise in salary, putting him in charge of a group of workers. Under this man's leadership, production improved immensely, and the problem was solved.

It had been difficult for Everette raising his sons alone. He had done without many things to provide for them, most of his paycheck went to settle the bill at the corner convenience store where he had an arrangement with the owner to let the boys have whatever milk, bread, or other groceries they needed. Now he had a partner, and we were happy raising our sons together.

Our boys were too young for the service during those war years, but the family upstairs had servicemen stationed away from home. Whenever they were shipped overseas, their pregnant wives returned home to "mama," and the family grew in leaps and bounds. Babies and puppies were too numerous to

Come Live With Me

count, and soon the family did not have enough room upstairs with babies crawling and puppies running everywhere. When they moved out, we were left with five unfurnished rooms and little money to buy furniture. We used a wine taffeta quilt that looked pretty good on one side to cover the back seat of an old car the boys had. Together we covered buttons, fluffed up the padding, and turned out a lovely loveseat. It was a perfect match for the round banana crates we padded and covered as chairs. Everette watched in awe and praised me. "Keep up the good work you and the boys are doing, and you will make professionals of them someday." Neither of us knew at the time what skilled workmen our sons would become.

Surprisingly, there was a demand for those rooms even before we finished furnishing them. A call came from the Diesel School in South Richmond which needed places for young servicemen during their thirteen-week training to bring their wives. We were able to accommodate three couples at a time, each having a bedroom and sharing the kitchen, bathroom, and living room—with its loveseat and matching chairs. This arrangement was fortunate, making it possible for us to gradually accumulate other furniture and to begin saving a little money.

Then misfortune came. While working on a construction job Everette fell through a building and broke his collarbone and arm. Although he received workman's compensation, the permanent damage to his arm made him unable to do construction work again. This was a painful experience for all of us. Yet I continued to believe that whenever one door is closed God opens another. Good fortune came when Everette, on his way home from a dental appointment, stopped by the streetcar barn to chat with some of the boys he knew there. Before leaving, he had been offered a job driving streetcars for the Transit Company. He was more than pleased and thought this was the best job in the world. Soon he was also training the new men who came to work there. Most important, our boys were growing up strong and had blended into a congenial family.

In time other good fortune came our way, and I found

myself eager to move again. Everette was working the day I met a lady who wanted to sell her rooming house on West Grace Street. With bedrooms on the second and third floors, it amply accommodated the sixteen girls who were living there. She asked me to buy it with all the furniture and let the girls continue rooming there. The offer excited me so much that I could not sit still waiting for Everette to come home. I caught his streetcar and rode around talking to him. Everette listened, making all of his regular stops while I talked nonstop. At the end of the line, I reversed the backs of the seats for him, and Everette stepped outside to change the position of the trolly for the return trip. Riding along again, I continued talking. Then as he often did, Everette told me, "If it makes you happy, I'm with you."

The way Everette said that always made me feel good, and I left the streetcar to begin packing for our move to Grace Street.

Come Live With Me

CHAPTER VII

*The house on Grace Street, filled with charm,
Became our home, loving and warm.*

"Everette, the kitchen walls have brown flowers."

"No, Grace, the walls are yellow and there are no brown flowers. I looked today." Together we went by that night to check on the Grace Street house again. When we turned on the kitchen light the "brown flowers" scampered to the cracks!

"I hope you are not moving any fine furniture here before you take my old bed out." One of the roomers added to our horror. "It is loaded with bed bugs." The exterminators were quickly called!

On moving day the old furniture was taken to the garage and the mattresses and box springs to the dump. We were pleased that the sixteen roomers chose to stay on with us, and like our boys, the girls were soon calling us Pop and Grace. We continued the arrangement of not serving meals for them, but Pop noticed that the girls always waited after work for Billie Ann to come home before they went out to eat together. I found out that this delicate little girl with the most beautiful eyes and blond hair never seemed to get enough to eat. The other girls saw that she had seconds by passing their extra bread and desserts to her. Still she remained tiny.

Everette decided he would help. "When I get my vacation

I'm going to cook a meal and fill Billie Ann with all the food she can eat."

Our table service was for six so Pop arranged for Billie Ann to sit at the head of the table and have a full meal with each group of five girls. Billie Ann surprised all of us as she ate, ate, and ate with all three groups, and the girls were delighted. They asked Pop, "Why don't you quit your job and cook for us?" I was surprised at his answer.

"Well, I used to be a cook for two hundred men in the army back during the first World War." The girls continued to praise Everette's cooking, and later that night he and I talked about the possibility of this new idea. Everette thought it might pay off as well as give him more time with the boys at night. He was working a lot at night and had been feeling the boys needed him at home then.

The very next day I began checking on health regulations, license, and improvements we would need to make. Everette thought we could take down part of the wall to the pantry and put a chopping block there with a window to serve through. I agreed. "What a great idea!"

After Pop went to work I asked the boys about helping me. They were willing and stood ready to help when I sawed right through the wall and pipe! It was the main sewer pipe and water flew in every direction. I rushed upstairs to the bathroom above and cut the water off, closing that bathroom from use until repairs could be made. The next day Pop was off from work, and in his usual calm manner he called a plumber to fix the mess I had made.

The girls were so anxious for good home-cooked meals they encouraged Pop and me by telling us, "Don't give up, you two will make a nice kitchen there."

Back to work we went on the project, and soon we were off to buy dishes, pots and pans, silverware, and glasses. Of course, I thought of crystal and sterling and went shopping at Miller & Rhoads, the fine department store downtown. Pop did his shopping at the Spotless Store, the popular hardware store, buying a huge rolling pin and heavy stoneware plates, bowls, cups and saucers like the Army and Navy use. These dishes were a glazed white with a green stripe around the edges. Back home I unpacked my beautiful table linens and crystal glasses, displaying their delicate beauty for Everette to admire. He took out his cup and saucer, picked up one of my sparkling glasses and dropped both on the floor at the same time. The glass scattered into a hundred pieces while the cup just rolled around on the floor and turned up beside the broken saucer. He had made his point,

and the next day I reluctantly returned my fine china. Emphasis on the practical side of this new venture took first place over my love of beautiful table settings. Yet I had to admit the dishes Everette chose were attractive.

Pop and I became a real team then. With our newly remodeled kitchen, we met all of the state health requirements and began serving daily meals. Pop was an expert organizer, and together we worked smoothly, planning the menus, cooking large quantities of healthful food, and serving delicious meals to our own boys and to the sixteen girls at a regular time. Even with this full schedule we kept our sense of fun and our reserved seats at the ballpark, rushing to arrive before the first ball was pitched each evening. Soon we were feeding dental students from the Medical College of Virginia and others who came each Sunday for an "all you can eat" dinner at $1.00 per plate. We had sixty-three regular boarders and served over one hundred meals on Sundays. Everyone on the block wanted to eat with Pop and Grace as our reputation continued to grow.

During these busy years our sons were growing too. Claude, the youngest, finally began gaining weight after tipping the scales at forty-seven pounds for almost three years. Those had been anxious years when the school called in a nutritionist, and his health was monitored regularly. Now he was catching up with his brothers. Claude loved to build and made especially fine bird houses. All of the boys used some of the furniture stored in the garage for woodworking projects. Birdhouses were made from drawers, and braces were made to straddle the fishpond whenever there was a need to back cars over it to work in the garage.

One day an antique dealer came by to pick up one of the dressers in the garage. The former owner had left it by mistake, and I had readily agreed she could send for it. When I took the dealer out to the garage he was astonished. "My goodness, look what you have here!" He raved about the furniture. "How much would you take for this?"

"Make me an offer." I was surprised when his first offer was more than I had paid for the whole lot. I thought of the pieces I had already given away and quickly agreed on the price. Then as the furniture was moved out, we kept searching for one of the deep drawers missing from an old wardrobe. It was finally spotted—perched up on a pole with a bird building her nest on it!

"You will have to wait until the birds hatch and fly away." The boys gave that order.

Laughing, the dealer hauled everything else away, paid me, and came back later for the drawer. His comment pleased me. "Your boys show great workmanship." I felt a worker with valuable antiques was certainly an excellent judge, and I remembered when Everette had said our boys would become good woodworkers. The marble top table I kept for our own use would always remind me of how dear our sons became during those full happy days together. My heart echoed a phrase from the twenty-third Psalm, "my cup runneth over."

Each of the four boys was gifted in many creative ways.

Sometimes they used their talents to convey their love and affection. One spring Robert gave me a very special hat for Easter. He had designed and made it himself while working after school as an errand boy at the Cavalier Hat Company. I promised to wear it every Easter until it wore out, a promise I kept. The newspaper featured a picture of me wearing the same perky straw hat many years after the boys had grown up. The years slipped by as the boys finished school and moved on to marry or serve in the Army.

By natural maternal instinct I was especially close with our sons and also with all the girls who came to live with me. I tried to fill their need for a second mother. They could talk to me, I would listen and offer advice if asked, but never betrayed their confidences. Many of the girls became like family to me, and when they eventually left I felt heartbroken. Yet I knew they had to make it in the world and that they were better equipped for success and happiness after the time spent in our home. This was gratifying to me and Pop. The girls often cried when they left, hugging me with warmth of affection and appreciation for the home away from home that Pop and I had given them. Some would return, and others kept in touch. Rereading their cards and notes, which I lovingly kept, was like sunshine to me, making my busy days lighter.

As the original girls moved or left to be married, many more were waiting to take their places, and we worked from this waiting list. One day the Green sisters called. "Can we add another sister to your list?"

The two sisters who were already living with us and working in Richmond had gone home for their mother's funeral. Now they needed to bring their young sister and take care of her. I felt a pang at the remembrance of my own loss long ago on the farm. Of course, I accepted the third sister, and the three Green sisters slept in the same double bed. They were all small, and it was hard to tell them apart. These beautiful girls were especially neat and kept everything in their room in place. After a short while the youngest sister became engaged to a young man in the service, but all three girls were always with him. Pop and I kept wondering which one he really liked best. The older sisters told the young serviceman that he had to take them along, or their little sister could not marry and go away with him to his next army base.

I stepped in to help with the wedding, sewing their dresses of light blue satin with tiny covered buttons. All were alike and all the same size, the lovely color making the Green sisters look radiant. As I watched them leave together after the ceremony in our home, festive with flowers, my heart filled with an aching tenderness for this family. The tears that filled my eyes overflowed because I knew I would miss them.

The room left vacant was soon filled with other lovely and loveable girls, but I began shedding tears more often—for no reason. My usual rosy glow had faded when Everette rushed me to the hospital in acute pain. This was the beginning of a long illness.

CHAPTER VIII

*After times of fear and illness,
A time of healing and kindness.*

The next three years were like a gray blur for me as I battled infections, one surgery after another, and hospital stays that included three of my birthdays in succession. During those times there was little birthday celebration, but I celebrated my faith in God. I believed there was a purpose for my life still ahead, and I never doubted that He would make me well again.

Everette was struggling without me to keep the meals going at home. His greatest help was Lucy, a black lady who lived in a nearby garage apartment. She was partially blind but an enthusiastic worker and a dedicated Christian. Lucy shared her faith and gift of healing with me whenever she visited me at the hospital. She was at my bedside the night the doctor came in again after hours. "Grace cannot live without an operation, and there is little hope she can live through the night."

Everette, frantically searching for blood donors, never gave up hope. Yet knowing I was desperately ill, he contacted the Red Cross to bring Charles home from his army base in Germany to see me.

Lucy leaned over my bed, comforting me with the words of the twenty-third Psalm, and then she laid her hands on me and prayed the most beautiful prayer I had ever heard. Though my body was in agony, I felt peace in my heart and a strong loving power filling the room. As I sensed this presence surrounding me, strength came like the gentle flow of a rippling stream, carrying me through that night of crisis. The next morning the doctor found me strong enough to undergo the needed surgery. He and Everette were both greatly relieved and amazed. Lucy was grateful but not surprised.

During my illness I was more disturbed about my boys than myself. The visit from my son, Charles, was a great comfort to me, but he had to return to his duty across the Atlantic Ocean. I began having nightmares about battlefields and Bernard, Everette's middle son, who was across the Pacific Ocean. There had been such a few years of world peace after World War II. Now serving in the army, Bernard was in the middle of the Korean conflict. Only the delicate sensitivity of a mother's intuition could explain how the realistic scenes of my dreams matched the real danger for Bernard. He and his infantry outfit were fighting their way to the Chungjin Reservoir. Withstanding attack after attack, they drove the Chinese back.

In my dreams I saw the gunfire. Distance could not break my close bond with Bernard. Like a mother hovering over her young, I dreamed I was an atom flying around protecting Bernard as he dodged the bullets from every direction ...

Most of Bernard's buddies were lost in the fight. Those surviving were cut off from supplies and had nothing to eat for four days. On the fifth day they made a break for it with the wounded in the trucks that would still run. With the Chinese close behind and in front of them, Bernard and others on foot left the road and went down to the reservoir, most of which was frozen solid. Bernard stepped on a part not frozen thick and fell up to his waist, his pants freezing stiff from the icy water. Trudging on, he was almost frozen when he was ordered to get on a truck, and he was given a blanket. Inside the truck as he tried to wrap up and get warm, he pulled off one of his boots ...

I had returned home from the hospital that week, but the nightmares continued for me. I saw Bernard rolling in the snow and nursing his frostbitten feet ...

The Chinese attacked again that night, turning most of the trucks over and killing the wounded men lying helplessly on the ground. Those who were able moved away from the slaughter. Some began to think of surrender, but "Never give up!" spurred Bernard on. He remembered those last words of advice that Pop had given him. Still shivering with only one boot on, he and a buddy cut across a snow-covered field, running awhile and walking awhile over miles of frozen terrain ...

In my nightmares I saw Bernard near collapse from exhaustion as he reached the safety of the marine division. I awoke crying ...

Later that morning I rode with Everette to mail our Christmas cards and gifts to Bernard. At the post office Pop talked with other parents who had word that only 140 of the 1200 boys in that unit had survived. Everette was terribly upset when he returned to the car, the cards and gifts still in his hands. "There is no use in mailing these, Grace." He was trying desperately to steel himself to accept the very probable loss of his son.

I was feeling weak, but my voice was strong. "No, no, Everette! I saw Bernard in my dream last night. I know he is safe." Everette looked at me for a moment, got back out of the car and mailed the cards and gifts. A short time later a letter arrived from Bernard. He had been taken by helicopter to a hospital in Japan where his recovery would require some months, but what a wonderful homecoming to which we could look forward! Awaiting his return, I painted a scene in shades of blue and white of the battle in my nightmares. When Bernard returned and saw the vivid details of my painting that matched the turmoil he had survived, he cried out in remembrance.

Many times during my convalescence I used my artistic talents to fill the empty hours. One Christmas season I decided to make our Christmas tree. This was before the wide popularity of artificial trees. My idea was to fashion a tree with pipe cleaners and wide packing wire, the kind used to wrap large crates. I acquired some of this from a nearby store, and Pop found me in the basement creating my wire fantasy around an iron tripod. He asked, "Honey, what are you doing?"

I answered simply, "I'm making a Christmas tree," and continued working along.

Everette took one look and went back upstairs. I heard someone ask, "Where is Grace?" and Pop's answer, "Better leave Grace alone; she has gone off her rocker."

Seeing the basement project, Robert, our oldest son, told Pop, "Laugh if you want, but Grace will make a beautiful tree if she puts her mind to it." And it was spectacular! Robert also admired my nature of fairness. I seldom took sides in any arguments that came up, gently smoothing the rough edges of both sides, if possible. "Miss Sweden" was his fond nickname for me.

In between more hospital visits I took walks in the fresh air to regain my strength. I loved to walk over to Monument Avenue and admire the bronze and granite monuments that gave the wide cobblestoned street its name. My favorite Civil War heroes were those four in the first mile of the beautiful tree-lined avenue. Shady maple trees also lined either side of the wide medium strip of grass which divided the east-west traffic, three lanes in each direction. Like a graceful archway, the colorful leaves were ablaze in autumn, a bright change after the cool of summertime green which shaded the area through the summer months. I was not strong enough to walk a mile yet, but sometimes I walked to the very beginning of Monument Avenue at Lombardy Street and Stuart Circle. From this point, West Franklin Street began eastward to Capitol Square in the downtown business area of the city, and Monument Avenue began westward. In the middle of the intersection was an iron-fenced circle where the statue of General J. E. B. Stuart on his spirited horse faced north. The dashing young cavalryman, wearing his debonair plumed hat, looked east.

On the rounded "corners" of the circle, four distinctively different buildings added to the charm of this fascinating circle. To the northeast—St. Johns United Church, the northwest—

Stuart Court Apartments, to the southwest—First United Lutheran Church, and curving around the southeast "corner"— Stuart Circle Hospital which opened in 1913, taking its name from its lovely location.

The next circle was one block west on Monument Avenue at Allen Avenue. Here the famous statue of General Robert E. Lee on his faithful horse, Traveller, faced and looked to his beloved South. Four blocks beyond this first statue to be erected, was the elaborate memorial to the President of the Confederacy. The impressive design of this monument provided a background for the statue of Jefferson Davis, standing with his right arm outstretched to the east. Thirteen columns, spaced several feet apart, swept around him in a semicircle. The memorial had been erected by the people of the South "in honor of their good leader, commemorating their love for the man, their reverence for his virtues, their gratitude for his services." This was inscribed on the outside of the semicircle.

Sometimes I could almost hear Davis speaking the eloquent

words of the inscription in the granite directly behind him: "Not in hostility to others, not to injure any section of the country, not even for our own pecuniary benefit; but from the high and solemn motive of defending and protecting the rights we inherited, and which it is our duty to transmit unshorn to our children" (Jefferson Davis, U.S. Senate, January 21, 1861).

This memorial gave me a sense of pride—certainly not pride in the great conflict of the last century that divided my country—but in the fact that those noble southerners who defended my native state had met the challenge to reunite the nation in 1865. The history of those tragic times intertwined with my own family history. Though I never knew if there was a direct line, I had been told that the Davis descendents on my mother's family tree were related to the brother of the president. I did know, and was more fully aware daily that many conflicts remained after all those years. Often my thoughts clouded the day as I strolled along. I pondered how war could change laws, but only God could change the hearts of people.

Three more long blocks west along Monument Avenue was the "Stonewall" statue. Here at North Boulevard, General Thomas Jonathan Jackson commanded the circle, both he and his horse, Little Sorrel, looking north to Broad Street. I seldom made it that far, but I enjoyed looking at all the different homes built considerably close to each neighboring house, their unique designs and dimensions complementing each other. The homes were separated from the street by a wide cement sidewalk and a very small front area of grass and shrubbery. Whenever I neared the house of my childhood daydream, I would pause. It always seemed to call out to me, "Come live with me." I had never completely given up on that dream, and I read with interest articles about the local controversy which surrounded the house at that time. There was much discussion and opposition to a proposed plan for its use as an alcoholic rehabilitation center. I often wondered how it looked on the inside now.

One afternoon I ventured up on the porch of "my house." Through the uncurtained windows I could see several people in the living room. They were sitting by the fireplace around a coffee table cluttered with bottles and glasses. Curiously, I peered through the stately glass door, trying to see the condition of the interior. For a moment I was the little girl of long ago again. Where were the red chair and the kind butler?

Suddenly the door was flung wide, and a young woman glared at me. "Why don't you come on in and have a darn good look!" Too startled to explain, I retreated home. Silently the old dream remained in my heart.

Deep x-ray treatments were the final therapy for my illness. I returned from the hospital weak but rejoicing and looking ahead. One morning Pop brought my coffee and the newspaper to my bed and sat down to read the menu for the day to me. I opened the paper and saw: "For sale, lovely old home on Monument Avenue, needs repairs." There was a short description and phone number but no price or other information.

"My house! My house is for sale! Everette, we can buy my house! We can have room for all the girls on the waiting list to come live with us." My daydream of thirty years ago had surfaced with the possibility of its fulfillment more real than the night I had dreamed in the red velvet chair with the lion's claws. Like a pleading child, I looked at Everette anxiously.

Come Live With Me

CHAPTER IX

There in all majesty it stood,
Still my dream, and he understood.

Everette put the menu down and looked over at me in disbelief. His eyes were kind as he stared at me propped up in bed. "Do you mean after all you have been through with your illness that you still want that old house?"

"Oh, yes! I have always wanted that house, and it has been waiting for me!"

"But, Grace, that old house will be nothing but work. Our home here is beautiful now. You have made it so lovely. Every time you take the draperies down people stop by and ask to buy the house. You have accomplished your dream. The girls are happy here, our boys are married, and we could continue living comfortably and save money for retirement as we had planned."

"I know, but I have my money now to buy it, and we could have so many more girls there who are waiting to live with us. And I have always wanted that house!"

"You really still want that old house?"

"Yes." I looked at Everette, my eyes filling with tears. "With all my heart!"

Everette shook his head and mumbled to himself, "If it makes her happy, I'm with her." He walked over to the small desk in the hallway, sat down and wrapped his long legs under the desk, fumbled with the lamp by the phone and dialed the number as I read it out to him. I listened intently as he spoke into the phone.

"Yeah, that old house on Monument Avenue you have advertised—what is that white elephant selling for now?" Everette repeated the price and I knew we could afford it. Yet I heard him bargaining.

"What! That old nightmare needs a lot of repairs. I am a builder myself and worked on that hand-carved woodwork years ago. My father put all that cedar storage area there. Yes, that's right, he was a Baptist minister, and when he wasn't preaching the word of God he was an expert carpenter. I remember helping him in that house. It has thirty-one rooms and eight baths and a large yard. Looks more like a castle, has about eighty windows."

I had never hear Everette talk about the house or that he had ever been in it. I just wanted him to say he would buy it at the price quoted. Instead Everette was making an offer of a price much less. "Okay, if that's not negotiable, we'll forget it. Those old houses are expensive to repair." Everette left his name and phone number and hung up the phone.

I was upset at his bargaining. "The owners will never accept that cut in price." I was so upset I covered my head and cried. "I have my money now, but the house will never be mine. I know they won't ever call back."

Everette tried to reason with me. "You can always go up on a price offer, but you don't ever go down to bargain. We will need the difference in their price for repairs anyway." He went on to the kitchen, busy with cooking, and organizing the tables. Like in his army training he kept everything clean and in order. Later I heard him answer the phone.

"Yes, we are planning to buy a large house on Monument Avenue, and we will have room for you. You mean Baptist Hall is closing, and all of you will have to move?"

Hearing this, I stopped crying and started praying that I could say, "Come live with me" to all those girls. Like an answer to my prayers, the phone rang several days later. Pop came in to tell me the owners would consider our offer if we settled before the end of the year. "Are you able to go down to their office tomorrow?"

I did not know if I was able to cross the room, but my answer was instant. "Yes, yes, of course!" It was already December, and snow and ice covered the ground. There would be so much to do. I did not have time to wait until I was able. After all, I had waited all my life for this house! Yes, I would be able!

That afternoon a neighbor came by and I excitedly told her about the house we planned to buy. The neighbor did not share in my enthusiasm. "There have been several millionaires who have been unable to make it there. Why do you think you can make anything of that old house?" Her remarks made me somewhat discouraged, but they did not discourage Everette.

"That does it! We are bound to go up because we are at the bottom, and up is the only way we can go." Everette was determined.

Buoyed by Pop's optimism, I managed to get myself ready the next morning. In fact, I dressed up and wore my sparkling jewels because this was such a special occasion for me. I looked at Everette who was neatly dressed as always but wearing his everyday tan khaki trousers and open-collar shirt. "Are you going like that?"

"I'm ready." Pop started toward the door. "Come on, hon', we have a house to buy at ten o'clock."

There was a doctor in charge of the sale. He was one of four who had formed a corporation to own the house. At the meeting he seemed more concerned about my physical condition than our ability to pay. I assured him I was in tiptop shape. Well, I felt like I was on tiptop of the world. I was buying my dream house! Everette made the conditions of the sale to include repairs the city code would require for the dormitory we planned to maintain. After a satisfactory contract was agreed upon, Everette rushed me home. He had cooking to do!

Inspecting the house was disappointing. Its run-down condition and the bottles and trash that littered every room almost overwhelmed me. The magnificent house of my dreams was such a wreck, I began to wonder it if could be restored. Comparing it with our present orderly home, I asked myself, "Why are we doing this?" My house on Grace Street was warm, but there was no heat in the Monument Avenue house as we cleaned and worked on the repairs. Everette was filled with energy and encouragement as he worked. This had become his dream too.

"Come on, Grace, let's get this job done. It is our dream, and we will have such a happy time here."

Somehow we did, and each day was happier as moving day approached. Everette and I took inventory of our furniture and the additional rooms we would need to furnish. Then we ordered seven thousand dollars worth of beds, mattresses, springs, and dressers. We spent several more thousand for linens, fans, and lamps. Echoes rang from the bare floors so carpet and rugs were also ordered.

The excitement was contagious among the girls when they were allowed to choose their rooms. This was done not by age but by length of time they had lived with us. The stairway was such a delight with its wide platforms where windows let in the light. Continuing to the third floor in the same pattern, it offered them a wide choice of spacious rooms which opened off a large center hall. The rooms gleamed with fresh paint and wallpaper. They were arranged for full privacy, facing the front, rear, and both sides of the yards. Some had connecting baths, and all had high ceilings and large windows that made them light and airy.

I kept the sewing machine humming, making colorful curtains for the rooms. My knack for decorating helped to make every room a beautiful choice for the girls.

The time came to contact those on the waiting list, and I found many young ladies between eighteen and twenty-five years of age anxiously waiting to come live with me. There were forty girls who moved with us into our Monument Avenue home in January of 1953. With Everette in charge, it was the smoothest move the moving company had ever experienced. The girls had

breakfast on Grace Street, and each girl stripped their beds that morning. Our faithful laundry man took the linens off, returning those from the previous week to our new home. Every piece of furniture was labeled as to where to be set up. It went so smoothly, the movers were surprised when they were finished. "We don't mind moves like this," they told us.

Pop and I served dinner in our new dining room, and with the arrival of all the girls, the rooms beamed with light and laughter. Afterwards everyone buzzed around putting their things in order, except Helen who worked a late shift at DuPont. She was already asleep when Pop decided he would clean off the awful grease from inside the chimneys that we might safely enjoy the fireplaces. He lit a candle to see inside, and the chimney caught on fire. Bright orange blazes rose from the tall chimney, and I remembered Helen asleep in the room upstairs by the chimney. I ran to Helen's room. "Get up, get up, the house is on fire!"

Pop ran to call the fire department. Eleven pieces of

equipment came clanking to the house and about twenty firemen swarmed the area. With this three-alarm welcome all the neighbors knew we were on the block, but we were not welcomed by all of them at first. It had been rumored that seven millionaires, five of which were multi-millionaires, lived on that block of Monument Avenue, and some of them had gotten a petition to have us moved out. Neighbors bought vicious dogs and made houses for them behind high fences. Undaunted, Pop made friends with the dogs before the owners and their dogs made friends. He used a little trick of buttering his fingers and the dogs liked him! The owners ended up calling Pop to quiet the dogs before they could enter their own yards.

It wasn't too long before we received a letter of welcome to the block, and many of our neighbors began enjoying the parties at our new home. I overheard them say, "We had our doubts that the Baldwins could keep up with the Monument Avenue pace. Now we are wondering if we can keep up with the Baldwins." Happily, we became known and loved as Pop and Grace of the Baldwin House.

THE BALDWIN HOUSE
2312 MONUMENT AVE.
RICHMOND, VA.

Home away from home for young business ladies

"POP & GRACE" BALDWIN

CHAPTER X

*We lived our dream, and all the girls
That came were like a thousand pearls.*

"The Baldwin House has the prettiest and the best girls in the whole world!" Everette often boasted about our girls. "America is the greatest country in all the world. Virginia is the best state in our great United States. Richmond, its beautiful capital, is the best city. Monument Avenue is the loveliest street, and the cream of the crop lives at the Baldwin House."

His little speech always made me proud, and it made the parents confident about their girls living there. The girls themselves felt cherished with a strong sense of security and self-worth. There were rules that reinforced this harmony. One of the rules was necessitated by the first and only serious disagreement among the girls at the Baldwin House. Surely there is no fury like a woman fighting for her man, and this was one hair-pulling fight. It began because one of the girls answered the phone when her roommate's boyfriend called. This girl liked him too, and accepted a date to dinner with him. When she returned, her roommate flew into a rage.

"It's not fair! I had him first!"

After Pop separated the girls, we called a meeting. It was decided by all the girls that if a young man was dating a girl at the Baldwin House he could not date another girl living there. If his

Come Live With Me

first girlfriend left, he could come back and date another girl, but only one at a time. The boys liked this arrangement as much as the girls did.

Many of the boys brought their sisters and best girlfriends to live at the Baldwin House, knowing it was a well-supervised home. This rule remained one of the requirements to live there, and no more disagreements were noted among the girls. They were happy "loving their neighbor."

From then on there were regular Wednesday night rap sessions. This became a time to discuss any problems or needs such as light bulbs out, extra blankets needed, or other household improvements. Everette would read next week's menus, and I collected recipes from the new girls. We served ice cream and cookies in the summertime and donuts in the winter months with coffee or hot chocolate. All the girls wanted to be present for these meetings, and ten dozen donuts disappeared in a hurry!

There was another rule that was difficult for the girls at times, and that was not to eat in their rooms. Yet the many tempting desserts left in the refrigerator for them, if eaten in the dining room, helped them obey. There was usually a barrel of apples in the pantry for snacks also. Everette and I were both pretty good cooks, he with his army experience, and I had recipes from all the good cooks in the many homes in which I had lived. One aunt had made the best biscuits, another knew the secret of flaky pie crust, and I had mastered many others. A family recipe for ten multiplied by four would serve the forty hungry girls. They would often ask, "Who made this? It is delicious!"

Whichever one was asked took credit, saying, "I did," no matter who made it. Laughing, Pop and I worked together as a real team in harmony. On the days we served pie, there were so many different kinds requested, we had to narrow it down to four. After dinner on a pie night, there were four slices left in the refrigerator, one of each kind made that day. Everette and I had gone to bed in our downstairs bedroom behind the library when we heard the refrigerator door open. It was Mary taking a piece of pie which she ate in the dining room and then cut the lights off.

A short while later the lights went on again in the dining room, and Pop asked, "Who is that? Are you all right?"

"It's Mary. I'm okay, just eating a piece of pie here because I can't take it upstairs." A half-hour later the lights went on and soon back off again. This was repeated the fourth time. The next morning Pop asked Mary why she was up so late, and Mary explained. "When I came home, there were four slices of pie. I ate the custard, then I came back and ate the butterscotch. Later I came down to eat the cherry, leaving the chocolate. I wanted that too, but I waited until all the girls were home so I could ask them if they wanted that last piece of pie. After no one was interested I came back and ate the chocolate. They were so tempting. I really wanted to eat all of them at one time, but I didn't want to take more than my share."

Truly the cream of the crop, the girls were very courteous and considerate of each other, and their trustworthiness was illustrated in the honor system of the Baldwin House. The Coke machine there did not have a slot to change money. Pop put his money changer from his streetcar days on top of the machine with ten dollars in coins for their use. There was a stamp drawer for stamps and change. If the girls needed change for carfare or lunch they would take a quarter or more, but leave an I.O.U. There was never a penny short without the note saying who owed it, which they paid promptly.

Pop fully trusted the girls, and they in turn trusted him to fix anything that broke. One evening when he was napping in his easy chair in the very spot where I had first dreamed in the red velvet rocker, he was awakened. The girl standing before him was a brilliant student.

"Pop, I can't get the washer to run."

Pop yawned, "Did you put your money in?" He reached in his pocket and gave her another quarter. "Try it again."

She soon returned, "Pop, I still can't get the washer to go."

"Well, what did you do to jam it? Are you sure you put your money in the slot?"

"Of course. You know I wouldn't cheat you of twenty-five

cents, Pop. I put every single penny in." Everette stood up, shaking his head, and started down to unclog the pennies.

I used a very simple bookkeeping system for the room and board payments. Marking the date, amount, and period of time covered whenever a girl paid, I would have her sign the line in her page. At the end of each year those books were kept, not only for tax purposes, but for their value in loving memories of each girl.

Some of the students lived at the Baldwin House on scholarship. It was Everette's idea that we give room and board free to ten percent of our girls. These were usually students recommended by the schools and deemed to be in need financially. There were local and out-of-state girls as well as Japanese and other foreign students who were chosen. The deserving four from the forty each year were never revealed to the other girls. All were treated in the same manner. Everette felt this was a way he and I could give our tithe to God at a time when we were not attending church regularly.

The size of the Baldwin House with its thirty-one rooms and eight bathrooms might have made it appear to be an impersonal building, but the warmth and caring of the girls who lived there gave it a family atmosphere that encouraged individual privacy as well as a wonderful comradery. Pop and I were like loving parents to the girls. We were very protective, and Pop made it a point to stay up until eleven before locking the door each night. The girls often laughed and said, "Pop can be asleep in his chair but still know who goes out and who comes in." Yet he respected each girl's freedom, and she was given her own front door key.

The girls came from far and near and loved their home away from home. There were many girls at all times and over one thousand girls through the years. They traveled from almost every state to attend college and business schools in Richmond. Some were cousins of governors, granddaughters of doctors, and daughters of delegates. There were those who arrived with all they owned in a shoe box with a book strap around it, and others who came with fine jewelry and fur coats. We installed a safe at the Baldwin House for the storage of these valuables. Pop and I were often surprised seeing the girls pack to leave with many bulging boxes of silver, china, and beautiful clothes which they had accumulated. It indicated they had been most successful in their schooling and job opportunities while living with us. Even more pleasing was the way all of the girls blended into a friendly group, their genuine friendships continuing long after they left.

The supreme reputation of the Baldwin House gained the approval of the board of education and recommendations from many private schools. Some of the faculty began telling students, "If you want a good job, tell them you live at the Baldwin House."

Of course, the house and I came under close scrutiny regularly. Dressed in my white uniform, I welcomed inquiring visitors to my home. It was the fulfillment of my childhood dream having girls come live with me at a time when they needed a home, encouragement, and supervision. Having never forgotten how I had longed for those things in my difficult years, I wanted the best for all the girls now. With Pop strongly supportive, I went about my duties joyfully, and those who came to check on conditions at the Baldwin House found nothing lacking.

Anne, a lovely girl from North Carolina who came to Richmond to go to school, wanted to stay at the Baldwin House. Her grandmother had left a trust fund for her education, but in order for the bank to pay her room and board from that fund, a most thorough investigation had to be made at the Baldwin House. Undaunted, I satisfied every question they could ask. When the final okay came through, Anne triumphantly proclaimed me "Woman of the Year."

Then the personnel staff from the Division of Motor Vehicles had a visit to interview me and to tour my home. Afterwards they went out to all the high schools in the state and hired the most qualified girls for employment in Richmond. They recommended the Baldwin House as the ideal place for the girls to live. Since the DMV Broad Street office was located only a

Come Live With Me

few blocks away, the girls could easily walk to work.

Soon I was approached by Dean Frank Pitts of the Medical College of Virginia's School of Pharmacy. With so many women admitted into their school at that time, they were searching for a wholesome environment for the students until a new dormitory could be built. Baldwin House passed the test again, and now more girls in white uniforms were filling the rooms and studying into the wee hours of the mornings. Other girls in the medical field who were already living there were nurses, medical technicians, and x-ray technicians at the new Richmond Memorial Hospital on Westwood Avenue.

Barbara was training to be a beautician, and she also wore a white uniform. Early one morning James, her husband-to-be, stopped by to give Barbara a ride to her school. The girls were rushing down, some of them calling out their breakfast order, "Pop, I need a two-minute breakfast!"

Many of the girls simply preferred buns or cereal, but it was Pop's custom to serve their eggs to order. During a lull in the kitchen Pop walked out by the stairway and spoke to the young man waiting there for Barbara. As James bent down to sit on the bottom step, Pop gave him a warning: "You had better not sit there, son."

"Oh, it won't get my pants dirty." About that time more than a dozen girls in white came dashing down the stairs. James looked up and quickly jumped up and out of the way. "Great day, it must be recess in Heaven. Look at all the angels coming down!"

One of our long-time "angels" first came as a visitor. While still in high school in Wisconsin, Jane had come down to visit her brother at Fort Lee Army Base in Virginia, and she was staying with his wife in nearby Petersburg. She came over to Richmond with this sister-in-law to visit a friend at the Baldwin House. They were invited to eat with the girls as it was the Baldwin House policy that our girls' visitors from out-of-town be guests at dinner. Like "Come live with me," I always said graciously, "Come eat with us."

Come Live With Me

Jane was so impressed with the hospitality of the southern mansion that she asked Pop, "When I graduate, can I come live with you?"

A wide grin spread across Pop's face. "Sure, Jane! Put your name on the list."

Later Pop told me, "Don't bother to call Jane. She is so far away she will have forgotten all about us." To our surprise, the next year Jane came back to live with us, and she always held a special place in our hearts as we did in hers. Jane was such a sweet young girl, smart as a whip, and had no trouble getting a job. She was a bit chubby, but most popular with everyone. One evening when the girls were sitting around the table deciding what to wear to a party that was coming up, Jane looked over at Nancy.

"I want to wear a jacket like the one you have on, Nancy."

Nancy was a small neat girl. She said, "If you can get in this one by the party, I will give it to you."

Jane was bubbling with excitement. She yelled out, "Pop, did you hear that? Nancy is going to give me her jacket if I can get into it!" She started on a diet the next day and lost all the weight needed to fit into the jacket for the party. Nancy generously gave her the jacket, and Jane was so proud she never gained one pound back. Later her job took her away from Richmond for a while. When she returned, there were no vacancies at the Baldwin House, but she did not want to live anywhere else. She pleaded until we consented to build a bunk for her under the basement steps which she happily occupied until a room was available. Our special friendship continued after she moved away to Arizona.

It did not seem strange to me that several girls with the popular name, Nancy, came to live at the Baldwin House. It did become puzzling when two Nancy's with the same last name came the same day. I was only expecting one when I received a phone call from a Nancy with the same last name. I was not surprised when Nancy asked, "Can I come now and move in?"

"Of course, Nancy. Come on. There is a room ready for

you." This Nancy came and was unpacking when the expected Nancy arrived. It was like unraveling a mystery, but fortunately I had another vacancy that day, and both girls settled in good-naturedly. Pop helped solve the problem of their identical names by asking their middle names. "Nancy Rose" was fine, but the other Nancy did not like her middle name which began with an "O." She became "Nancy O." Both were happy and loved by all the girls.

The Baldwin House became even more beautiful through the years. It was like a medieval castle on the outside, but inside it was a warm, homey residence. The sense of right and goodness within, and the love of life and each other which the girls shared deepened its beauty. Barbara experienced that beauty when she moved there while studying to be a dental hygienist. Babs, as she was usually called, came from Pennsylvania. At nineteen, it was her first time away from home for any length of time, and she was terribly homesick. I could remember my own homesickness, and of course I understood. In turn, I tried to be kind and gentle to comfort Babs. After adjusting to being away from home, Babs came down with the flu, and she was too weak to make it up and down the stairway from the third floor for meals during her recovery. It was all in a day's work for me, bringing soup and encouragement up to Babs' room, but my doing that cheerfully meant a lot to her. Always trying to have time for the girls' needs left little time for myself. Yet this was my dream come true, and I was happy living it out fully—with Everette's strong support.

Ours was a bond that grew stronger with each day we worked together. Everette was definitely the chief chef and kitchen organizer, but he was never above sitting and peeling a bushel of potatoes or taking over the dishwashing for me if our help failed to show up in time. I was his helpmate, taking orders, and serving the meals, baking pies, as well as arranging for the new girls who came and helping them get settled in their rooms. I was also fully capable in the cooking arena as the girls learned one evening when dinner tasted exceptionally delicious. They discovered Pop had been sick and I had cooked the entire meal. My decorating skills improved with my own enjoyment, and throughout the house my paintings on the walls testified to a special pastime I loved. I often wondered if my parents would be proud of their little farmer's daughter, and I hoped always that the way I used God's gifts would be pleasing to Him.

Come Live With Me

CHAPTER XI

Laughter, tears, and telephone calls,
And music echoed in our halls.

The good times rolled, and the bad times mixed with the good. Life at the Baldwin House was like life in most families. We laughed together through the happy times and pulled together through the difficult times. We leaned on each other in tragic times, and the closeness of friendships strengthened the girls. Each girl grew in spirit and gained in character from the experiences they shared. Watching this beautiful process, Everette and I felt a deep admiration. Hopefully our home was providing a stepping stone into the world for our girls.

Even though most days were long and demanding, the years were adding up to a successful dream for Everette and me, a full life in which we both had such a happy time together. When Everette bought his dream car, the girls squealed with delight. The shiny gold Cadillac was so roomy and luxurious everyone had to have a ride. Like with the other girls, Pop was like a second daddy to a precious young girl from down near the Chesapeake Bay in Mathews County. She did not hesitate to ask him a big favor.

"Pop, when I get married, will you drive me to the church in your gold Cadillac?"

Proudly Pop promised that he would. "I will get a chauffeur's cap and take you there in style."

"Oh, no, Pop! I don't want you to dress like a chauffeur. I want you and Grace to sit in the front together, and I will ride in the back dressed in my wedding gown and veil."

When the promised day arrived, Everette and I gladly made the three-hour trip to Mathews and drove the radiant bride to the church from her home. We were like family at her joyous wedding, a special time to be lovingly remembered.

Another time to be remembered was not so special. It was October of 1954, when an evil wind blew Hurricane Hazel into the Richmond area. Residents had been forewarned that this hurricane would be making a path through the city, and Everette saw that all the windows and doors of Baldwin House were anchored as securely as possible. The girls were asked to bring their bedclothes downstairs where they made a huge pallet on the floor away from the windows. When Hazel tore furiously through the Monument Avenue area, many windows were broken, and glass was scattered everywhere. Of course, the power went out, and the night was spent in darkness and anxiety. The only lights were the gas lamps that we had installed to illuminate the pathway along the side yard. Beyond the lamps were a row of tall slender Lombardy poplar trees. The lamps flickered in the wind and rain as the disaster of the night wore on. The girls and I huddled together, lying still but hardly sleeping as the fierceness of the wind's strength shook the house. We heard a crashing sound and those who glanced out of the window screamed. Before our eyes the poplars were blown down, falling in a line, one on the other like a row of cascading dominoes. The girls huddled closer and prayed together. They were calmed and comforted by the faith shared through the unforgettable night.

Morning found trees uprooted and porch furniture blown into the wet streets cluttered with leaves. Worse still was the discovery that there was no water. Flooding from the storm had affected the city's water supply. Only a muddy trickle was available. It was not fit to drink. Fortunately, there was an artesian well in the backyard. Everette and I had been told about it when we bought the house, and we had used it to water flowers through the summers. The well had been dug when the house was being built because the property was beyond the city limits at that time. Water was necessary for construction, but by the time the house was completed city water became available and the well was capped off.

Now Everette connected the long garden hoses, and the girls helped carry them up the fire escape at the back of the house, reaching the second and third floors. With the well water we were able to flush the commodes and fill the bathtubs. It also gave us water for drinking and cooking. This was such clear clean water! Our frightening experience became a time of thankfulness.

A true tragedy touched all the girls when infantile paralysis invaded our lives. There was no cure for the dreaded disease caused by a virus which had crippled many, including the former United States President, Franklin D. Roosevelt. Polio, as it was known from the scientific name, anterior poliomyelitis, raged that summer. A group from the Baldwin House had escaped the heat of the city for awhile at a swimming lake outside of Richmond. Soon afterwards Rose suddenly developed the known symptoms of polio: fatigue, fever, nausea, headache, and muscle pain. This dear young girl was taken to the hospital immediately. She was placed in an iron lung, a breathing machine much like a huge body cast, but Rose died within a week. The entire household sank into sorrow with the loss of this beloved friend. The memory of Rose lived on in contributions to the March of Dimes which helped fund Dr. Jonas Salk's successful development and testing of a polio vaccine. This led to the perfection of a live virus oral polio vaccine by Dr. Albert Sabin. With nationwide vaccination in 1962, in which the Baldwin girls participated, the wide-spread occurence of this highly contagious disease was erradicated. Then polio was no longer a threat for other beautiful young "Roses."

Betty Jean was one of the several twins among the girls, her twin being a brother who lived in another area. Seeming to be perfectly fine one day, she suddenly began to cry out in distressful pain. Betty Jean told me she had an awful headache, like nothing she had ever known before. The throbbing pain had come on abruptly, and Everette's standard "take two aspirins" gave no relief whatsoever.

"Please do something! Do something! My head is coming off!" At that moment the phone rang, and Everette answered it downstairs. Upstairs was strictly the girls' domain, but this time Pop climbed the stairway to bring the sober message that explained Betty Jean's violent headache: her twin brother had been killed instantly in a head-on automobile collision the hour before. The shocking news spread through the house, and the girls came with love and sympathy for Betty Jean. As her tears flowed the intensity of her headache subsided. Support from the girls was a great comfort to her. Their own understanding, in turn, gained deeper dimensions of family ties that bind and losses that separate.

There were other twins who lived at the Baldwin House. Those who were identical had great times confusing people, often switching dates as a joke. Cecilia and Elizabeth were full of fun. Tiny and trim with pretty blond hair, these twins fully enjoyed their jobs as models. When an assignment required them to dye their hair, the transformation was fascinating. Pop and I were amazed watching them leave for work one day with their new hair-dos, one pink and the other blue!

Florence was a vivacious brunette from Coles Point in the Northern Neck along the Potomac River. She taught school there in Westmoreland County and came up to live at the Baldwin House during several summers while completing her college education. When she first met Pop and me, Florence knew she had found her home away from home.

"I am a little country girl, and I have always wanted to live in a mansion. This is truly a beautiful one, indeed it is!" She loved being there, and she loved all the girls. Everette fondly called Florence our "goodwill ambassador" because she was always buzzing about trying to help the girls. Pop assured me,

"You don't have to worry about the new girls now that Florence is here. She will get them into activities."

Groups would attend the performances at Dogwood Dell and go to church together on the Sundays they were in town. Sometimes the girls were able to go home for the weekends, but as Jean, a quiet blond from Coles Point discovered when a snowstorm kept her in town, there were many fun things to do in Richmond. The girls had a grand time in their friendships whether at the movies, museums, or dances. They were wholesome, good outings together.

"Those who don't belong here will soon find out," Florence would explain to the girls. "The atmosphere at the Baldwin House is too good for evil to exist around it."

After her own Mother died, Florence told me, "You are my next best Mom." Hopefully, I had earned that sentiment from all the girls, for I tried daily to demonstrate the true character of a loving mother in my care and genuine concern for the girls. Both Pop and I were there for them in sickness and health, in troubles, and in happiness.

With or without our "ambassador," various outings were planned for all to enjoy, and Pop was always ready to help with transportation. One hot Saturday Pop made three trips to carry the girls to a picnic at the lake. Near time to return, several of the girls said, "Pop, we have a way home, but we won't be late."

This was not unusual because the girls were most popular. After two trips back, Pop and I had settled down at home when the phone began ringing, asking for the girls by name. I answered once, and a young voice sounded excited. "Who am I speaking to?"

"I am Grace."

"Yeah, Grace, I know you! You were the prettiest girl at the lake today."

"Who are you?"

"I'm Sarge."

Amused, I asked, "How did you get my number?"

"It's on the bulletin board here at Fort Lee. All of us met

Come Live With Me

some dolls at the lake today. They said the old man there runs such a tight ship, he won't let us come over without having a date. Since no blind dates are allowed, we are arranging dates in advance. A van of guys from the base want to come over tonight. Will you be my date?"

"Well, I'm the old man's wife." I laughed, and the boy hung up. He called right back.

"May I speak to Mary?"

Pop had answered this call. "Which one?"

"Either one will do." The flustered Sarge quickly hung up again.

"What's going on?" Pop had suspected something when so many calls were coming in only for the girls who went to the lake that day. He laughed because he remembered his own army days. "Okay, all of the girls that plan to see the soldiers, be dressed to come down to meet them."

Before dark the big covered army van drove up and parked on Monument Avenue. Eighteen young men filed out, shined their medals, spit on their shoes to polish them, straightened their caps, and came up to the door in an orderly fashion. Pop, waiting at the door, stepped out on the porch, and signaled "attention." The soldiers knew he had been an army man, and they saluted. Pop gave them a welcoming grin. "Come on in, boys. These are the Baldwin girls, and this is my wife, Grace. Which one of you is Sarge?"

"Him! We wouldn't let him come and spoil everything for us. He already made one big mistake. You do have a lovely wife, sir."

"Flattery will get you everywhere." As the foyer and adjoining rooms filled with the girls and young men, Pop asked, "How many of you play music?" He had moved over to the piano and picked up the trumpet, handing it to one soldier, the horn to another. One boy spoke up for the drums, another for the guitar, and Pop picked up the mandolin to begin the beat.

Our parties were always enhanced by music, Everette's lifetime love. Even on Grace Street our most pleasant evenings were spent around the Baldwin piano that had belonged to his mother. She had been organist at the Baptist Church where his father had preached. Everette's musical talents came from her, and he could play all the instruments which he kept ready to enliven any occasion. Tonight Pop was elated to have so many boys for his band.

The music flowed through the lighted rooms and out into the moonlight. Most of these young men were a long way from home, but they felt a warm welcome here that lifted their spirits. I filled the dining room table with cool refreshments, and it was not long before the Oriental rugs were rolled up, corn meal sprinkled on the parquet floors, and everyone joined in dancing. The spontaneity and congeniality of this party was unmatched. The couples danced and danced until midnight. There were bittersweet farewells, but not one girl left the house with anyone. They were so appreciative of the way Pop had allowed them to entertain the soldiers in a respectful manner. The boys left saying they would never forget the Baldwin House. Some of them carried their memories overseas. Their letters of thanks came from Vietnam, one with a postscript: "Recommending your home to my best girl."

Afterwards I could not help comparing this party with the first one there when I was a little girl. Again not one person had been my age, but this time I never knew a moment of loneliness. In my prayers I asked God to bless the girls and soldiers. He had more than blessed me!

Come Live With Me

CHAPTER XII

The sixties brought changes our way,
The dawning of a different day.

Music continued to be a part of life at the Baldwin House. It was played in many tempos. Marching songs were heard as the procession of girls came and went, the blues when moods were low, sonnets of love as sweethearts became engaged, and then the wedding march leading them to the altar. Some ceremonies were performed at the house and even more often, I hosted wedding receptions at the Baldwin House. The music of laughter accompanied light happy tunes heard in the everyday fun of friendships, and hymns of praise rang out for successes achieved. When the girls descended the stairway in their colorful evening gowns to be presented with flowers and escorted to proms and gala parties, it was like a symphony. Throughout the years was the recurring melody, "Come live with me."

For Everette it was a joyous aria when he heard Jane play the piano. She had come to the Baldwin House from her home in Crewe, Virginia. As Everette listened he remembered Edna, a pianist from Winchester, Virginia, whose musical talents had filled the Grace Street house with beautiful music when she lived there with us. He volunteered to buy the new sheet music Jane wanted, and I took her down to Walter D. Moses Music Store on Broad Street for her selections. Jane was completely fascinated with all the pianos and organs that were on display, and I found myself standing at the counter alone as the salesman trailed after the girl. He looked back at me and winked, "I know what she is looking for, and I have one near the back."

Suddenly Jane stopped and called, "Here it is!" I looked at the piano, but I did not see anything different about it. The salesman began giving his pitch as Jane sat down at the keyboard.

"Henry Steinway only autographed the finest pianos after he played them to his own perfect satisfaction. They are very rare today."

I was neither impressed nor interested enough to ask the price, but here the salesman was, giving me a pattern showing the actual shape and dimensions of the large piano the gifted girl was playing. I had only come to buy sheet music. As soon as Jane and I returned, Pop asked about the sheet music we had bought.

"Oh, Pop, you should see—and you should hear—the magnificent Steinway piano I played today. It has the most melodious tone! And this one is personally autographed by Henry Steinway. He only signed the finest pianos, and they are very rare today." Jane was almost breathless with admiration.

When I gave Everette the pattern from the salesman, he laid it on the floor in front of the bay window in the library. It fit the area perfectly, but Everette did not discuss the piano any more that evening.

The next day I had a doctor's appointment to which I walked because the office was near. Returning, I saw the Walter

D. Moses truck backed over the sidewalk and right up to my porch. Men were unloading that Steinway piano! Dollar marks flashed through my mind, and I wondered how many thousands of dollars it cost. When I came inside where the piano had been placed by the big bay window, there Everette stood, beaming. "Everette! How much did you pay for that?"

"Nothing! Not one cent! They will send a bill, " Pop laughed. "Before I married you, I tried to get a twelve-dollar guitar on credit, and they threw me out of the store. Today they sent me a five thousand dollar piano, and all I had to do was sign for it."

Standing there looking at the man I loved, I smiled. "If it makes you happy ..." How often he had said that to me. Of course, Jane was overwhelmed when she saw the Steinway awaiting her touch. How she reveled in playing it all the while she lived at the Baldwin House. It gave listening pleasure to all the girls, but Pop was the happiest!

A few years later my little granddaughter came to visit us, and Pop taught her to play chopsticks. He was thrilled at how quickly she learned to play it. "This child is really talented. If she takes lessons and learns to play well, the piano will be hers." As she grew, Deena played beautifully!

It was a wonderful scene when snowfall turned Monument Avenue into a winter wonderland. The morning sunshine on the white velvet sparkled like diamonds, but this pristine state of the yard never lasted long. The girls would bundle up in extra sweaters, woolen caps, gloves and boots, and race out to the untouched blanket of snow. Here they would fall, laughing, and swing their arms and legs to make snow angels. Then the "angels" pooled their energies to make the biggest snowman on the avenue. Their activities kept the bonds of friendships growing, and their appetites growing too!

Pop's dedication to feeding those appetites with enjoyable meals had always made mornings his busiest time. During the years on Grace Street when we had many boarders in addition to the sixteen girls rooming there, one of the boarders who lived close by stopped in often in the mornings. She would come right on into the kitchen, and she would rave about the delicious dishes Pop had made, asking how he cooked this and that. He tried to be pleasant and stopped more than once, patiently listing the ingredients and how to add them. After an especially great dinner, Pop was not surprised to see her the next morning. He was much too busy though to stop and answer her usual questions. Without missing a beat in his preparations he simply explained.

"There is nothing to it. Just add water and stir." This became a standing joke that the girls continued to laugh about even after our move to Monument Avenue.

The joke was remembered at the Baldwin House when the girls were planning a wedding shower for Jean, one of the sixteen girls from Grace Street who had moved with us to Monument Avenue. She had a large room and bath there on the second floor with Lorena and Louise, called "Lou." The three were lovely girls and the best of roommates. When Jean's wedding was coming up, Lorena and Lou planned her shower as a surprise on her birthday. John, the husband-to-be, took Jean out to dinner to celebrate, and to give the girls time to decorate. Afterwards he told Jean they had to stop back at the Baldwin House and give several of the girls a ride to the movies. Jean did not suspect anything because she knew John was good-natured and always willing to help the other girls.

Jean and John walked in together, and the surprise was such a happy one with all the girls showering her with gifts. One of

Jean's most prized gifts was a blank book in which to write her recipes. It was one of the dummy books made up before prospective books were bound at L. H. Jenkins Book Bindery on West Broad Street. These were later discarded, and a friend working there had retrieved this one for the shower. The title decorating the cover was POP'S FAMOUS RECIPES, and on the inside page was ADD WATER AND STIR. Remembering this little joke brought much laughter and added to the fun and happy memories of the shower. Jean's marriage to John was like a lived happily ever after story. Her husband was one of three fine young men named John who were often at the Baldwin House. Later Lou married one of them, and Dot married the other young John. Pop had a wonderful relationship with all the boys, and each one respected his strict code and enjoyed their music sessions with him. He gathered a crowd around the piano whenever the boys stopped by for their dates.

One Christmas a top-of-the-line recliner chair arrived for Pop with a card signed, "John." Neither Everette nor I ever knew which John had sent this super replacement for his old worn-out chair, or if all three of them had been in on the gift. We only knew it was a real tribute of love and respect, and we were deeply touched by it.

In contrast to the purity of the snow in the wintertime and the Christmas spirit of the holidays so joyfully celebrated, was a discovery in the bright freshness of a spring morning. It brought Everette and me a sense of foreboding, like a muffled alarm we did not want to hear. Walking out to gather a bouquet of flowers, I was puzzled by a dark heap of rubbish in the corner of the yard. As I looked closer, I was even more surprised at the assortment of empty bottles and beer cans. Stepping back from it in distaste, I called for Everette to come out and see this messy debris. "This has appeared overnight... who?" We did not feel our girls were involved, but we decided to call a meeting.

Before the girls came down to the living room, Pop arranged all of the bottles and cans on the mantle. He was very serious as he explained his concerns that evening. "I have had a detective check these bottles, and we can identify fingerprints from them. But ..." Pop hesitated as he looked at each of the girls, "If we never find another bottle or can in the yard, there will be no further investigation."

The girls were solemn. Hardly a word was spoken as they headed back up the stairway. I firmly believed the trash had been left by some outsiders who happened to be passing through the neighborhood and had lingered in the dark privacy of the surrounding bushes for awhile. My theory remained unproven, but nothing like it was found again. Pop, of course, cleared the mantle, and the incident was never mentioned again.

Everette and I became increasingly aware of a changing world that was sneaking into our lives at the Baldwin House. Like grains of sand in an enormous hourglass of the sixties, many differences became part of the times. Newspaper headlines attested to the more callous attitudes, looser standards, carelessness of dress, mistrust in authority, and an overall "me first" philosophy emerging, all sowing seeds of unrest and growing into rebellions on campuses and in work places. This was the decade when the hippie movement had its influence on teenagers still in school as well as young adults in a confused grown-up world. They were known as flower children in this time of freedom of expression.

The Vietnam War contributed many changes. There were so many pros and cons of this war that many servicemen were sent over there without ever knowing why they were there. Some believed they were saving democracy, but somehow full support was often lacking. It all ended without a feeling of victory. When these veterans returned, it was without a welcome home from the nation. I remembered the proud celebrations honoring Bernard and other soldiers when they returned from Korea. Now many Americans who had risked their young lives in Vietnam, a place few citizens could locate on a map, were received with contempt when and if they returned home. I would hear the girls discussing the hardened attitudes of boyfriends who returned. With self-esteems deflated, they sometimes became resentful of the independence the girls had gained in jobs that equalled positions traditionally only men had held. These changes strained their relationships.

We also marvelled at the many good changes which occurred during the sixties. On July 21, 1969, Everette and I were watching the television screen as it revealed the first man to walk on the moon. Everette was very impressed. "This is truly 'one small step for man and one giant step for mankind'. Flying was considered impossible when I was born. Then the Wright Brothers came along, and about 1903, they made and flew the first airplane. I remember Charles Lindbergh made the first transcontinental flight in May of 1927. Old Lucky Lindy! Now I can hardly believe that a spaceship has taken men to the moon. It is like something from the Flash Gordon comics. Here we are watching astronauts place the American flag where only the face of the man in the moon has ever appeared."

In those years of good and bad changes, nationwide church attendance began to decline. I felt a tinge of conscience that my own regular worship had begun to lag. My faith was still strong, but I realized the stability that religion or a belief in God had always offered had truly suffered with the new law disallowing prayer in schools. Many youths drifting in a sea of confusion had no anchor, no hope, no reason for a faith on which to hold. The very foundation had been legally pulled out, like a rug, from under their growing feet. With the increase in the divorce rate, many children growing up in the new age were from broken homes. They became latch-key kids, their mothers often working with little time as single parents to give their children deep roots, roots needed to hang on to in the turbulent sixties.

Remembering my own difficult years, I tried with all of my heart to be there for the girls. They often talked freely with me, and I kept their confidences. In their openness with me, new lifestyles confronting them were discussed. One that was becoming more widely accepted was the pill, the new oral contraceptive available to unwed women as well. Sometimes samples of these pills were easily obtained in the doctors' offices in which girls worked. The pill became the in thing to use. Old-fashioned abstinence was considered just that, out-of-date, by many in the dawning of this new age of sexual freedom. The resulting unwanted babies brought the beginning of the heated abortion controversy.

Being realistic, I knew some of the girls would follow the new wave of thinking, but I was proud that most of our girls continued to uphold their higher ideals. I never stopped seeing the inner beauty of each girl, and I looked beyond the tight jeans, mini-skirts, heavy makeup and unkempt hairstyles with love for all of them. Like most mothers with their children, I knew their many defects, but always believed them perfect.

In addition to the many innocent girls as yet unaware of the newest problem, drugs and narcotics, there were three "in the know" at the Baldwin House. Billie Jean, Dot, and Carolyn worked for the Federal Bureau of Investigation, and they often went out as undercover agents. At those times the FBI men, acting as guests, went along to protect the girls. The night a drug raid had been planned for a truckstop north of Richmond, two of the FBI girls went out on duty dressed in blond wigs, tight jeans, flashy sweaters and highly scented perfume. Before leaving the house, they called downstairs to us.

"We are coming down the back stairway for you to see us so you can identify us if there is unforseen trouble."

Everette and I would not have recognized our FBI girls disguised as prostitutes. A huge drug supply was seized, making this a most successful operation. Relieved when the girls returned safely late that night, I felt a quiet peacefulness settle over the Baldwin House. As I drifted off to sleep, I never dreamed how that peace would be disrupted by many unknown changes yet ahead.

CHAPTER XIII

Was it my pride that dealt the blow,
Or was God telling me to go?

The girls filled the Baldwin House with sunshine, and they filled their summer weekends with a diversity of activities. Mary and Scottie had planned for a day at the beach on a hot, sultry Saturday. The bright glare of the morning sun reflected from Scottie's shiny red convertible as he parked in front of the house. With youthful energy he jumped out and bounded up the steps to the doorway, barefoot and wearing only his bathing trunks, called "baggies" at the time. He rang the doorbell as Mary was coming down the stairway in her cool sundress and matching white sandals, carrying her beach towel and bathing suit in a bright canvas bag.

Pop had come in from the kitchen and opened the front door to Scottie, who stepped inside. "Is Mary ready?"

"Mary is ready, but you are not ready to take her anywhere. Where are your shoes and shirt? I'm not letting one of my girls leave here with a half-dressed man."

Scottie looked up at Pop, "Hey, we're going to the beach. Come on, Mary."

Mary walked over and stood between them. "No, I'm not going against Pop's rules."

"Aw, come on! You don't have to live here. You can

move."

"You want me to leave my home? No way! I like it here too much." Mary walked over and sat down in the living room. Scottie looked at Pop, who remained silent, and made a quick exit. Watching the convertible pull away from the curb, Mary reassured Pop. "It's okay. I don't want to disobey your rules, and I think Scottie should show a little more respect for me."

A short while later, the doorbell rang and Pop opened the front door again. There stood Scottie in his black tuxedo and

white tie! "May I take Mary out now?"

Pop could hardly answer him for laughing. "Sure, Scottie! That's more like it. I don't mind that you have gone to the extreme either. I am glad you think enough of Mary to respect my rules for the girls here." Mary and Scottie made a charming couple as they drove off to the beach with the top of the convertible down.

A few years later during a visit to my dentist, I had to laugh. Calling in the lab technician, the dentist introduced me to Scottie. Scottie's face lit up with a big grin. "I know Grace well. You haven't lived until you have been thrown out of the Baldwin House by Pop. He steered a tight ship, but he was always fair."

The dentist nodded in agreement. "I have a secretary who lives at the Baldwin House, and she loves it."

Everette was also very respected in the neighborhood. There was a great controversy about paving over the cobblestones on Monument Avenue. It was finally prevented by Mrs. Taylor, a prominent resident of the historic street that we wanted to preserve. She stopped the bulldozers by lying down in the middle of the cobblestoned street. Later the committee had to decide how to spend the money that had been appropriated for the paving no longer required. Pop was among several who suggested it be used to install underground irrigation that would keep the median strip green year-round. This unique sprinkler system greatly enhanced the beauty of Monument Avenue of which Everette and I were extremely proud.

The pride I felt in the Baldwin House increased as the success of my dream continued. We had made many improvements to the grounds. Of course, much credit was given our gardener, C. C., who was also a devoted friend, almost like a brother to Everette. I would walk through the well-kept yard, admiring the beautifully blooming shrubbery. Loving flowers as I had from childhood, I was especially fond of the tulip tree that bloomed so abundantly, and I loved the colorful Virginia creeper, my rose bushes and every delicate flower. Looking up at the sparkling windows which had been professionally cleaned, I admired the new draperies I had chosen and hung at the many windows. My thoughts were about all I had dreamed of doing and how Everette and I had accomplished that dream.

"I have come a long way from the daughter of a dirt farmer." My thought was true, and perhaps I had earned those material rewards. Yet deeper than any self-satisfaction in my heart was a feeling of praise and gratitude to God.

Knowing so well that God had been with me through my most difficult times, I knew He was ever beside me. Everette and I began each day with prayer together. Our full busy days kept us from regular church attendance and activities, but we strived to live our faith in God, serving Him daily. Only He could strengthen us for the crushing turn of events our future held.

It began one morning when Pop snapped at me as we served breakfast. We had never made any display of disagreements in front of the girls. Arguments between us were discussed only in the privacy of our room. Pop's outburst startled the girls and me. I was quick to come back at him. "What is your problem?"

"I'm not feeling well."

This was unusual for Everette, but I answered lightly. "Well, maybe you should see a doctor."

A hush came over the dining room as the girls waited silently. Not the slightest tinkle of silver or glass could be heard. Everette started back into the kitchen and lowered his voice. "Make me an appointment."

There was no animosity between us as I walked with Everette to his appointment later that day. He was cheerful, and I saw him into the doctor's office before returning home. Going about my usual duties, my thoughts were centered on the beauty of the rooms and the many material gains in my life when the phone rang. Answering it, I recognized the familiar voice of our doctor.

"Your husband is very ill, Grace. I am having an ambulance take him to the hospital right away." The solemn tone shook me. I asked which hospital and hung up. My knees were shaking so that I knelt down on them by the phone. The prayer I whispered was an urgent plea.

"Oh, God, please show me the way, and be with Everette." Tears were streaming down my face, and I felt the Lord's guiding hand lifting me back up and leading me out to be with Everette at the hospital. There in his room I was sitting beside him when Dr. Frank Kelly confirmed our fear. The disease was cancer, and the prognosis was not good. I stayed with Everette as much as possible while continuing to carry the full load at home. I was at his bedside one evening when he seemed very ill, and I was worried. Suddenly he sat up in the bed, fully awake.

"Lord, I know I am ill, and my days on earth are limited. I just want to get my house in order so my wife will be secure for her later years. Would you give me time to do that? How long? Two years? Thank you, Lord." Without a glance at me, Everette fell back on his pillow and slept soundly.

Much worried, I rushed back to see Everette the next morning early. I was surprised to find him sitting up, seeming to be better.

"What happened to you last night, Everette?"

"You tell me what happened, Grace."

"Well, you sat up and had a talk with the Lord. You asked him for time to get your house in order." I could not bear to tell my husband he only had two years to live since he did not seem to remember. I decided to add a zero to the two. "He gave you twenty years."

Everette did not comment. When he returned home he began meeting with his lawyer and making plans for me to remain financially secure when he would no longer be with me. He was well aware how difficult it had been for me to keep the house going without him even though I had hired additional help.

Leona was a real blessing during the years she worked at the Baldwin House. She not only knew how to keep everything in the gracious house in beautiful order, she had the special ability to direct the other workers. I could trust her fully to see that chores were done in the correct manner. The girls and their rooms were never neglected because Leona respected me and I respected her.

"I can tell you get to know each girl. That's what really makes this fine mansion such an upstanding home." We became real friends, and I wrote a poem for Leona about friends and prayer.

With determined efforts I continued my duties, comforted by Everette's presence for advice and support. Being physically unable now to share the work load as he had always done, Everette felt the joy fading from our dream. Together we had lived our dream happily, but the shortened span of his life was bringing changes. It was difficult making me see the reality that I could not continue with the Baldwin House without him.

"I know how dearly you love this place. You don't want to give it up, but I think it best, Grace. Since the house is clear of debt we can finance it and you hold the mortgage on it. I do not know, but I firmly believe that in three years' time the Baldwin House will be back on the market again. You could decide to buy it back then, but my advice is to leave it alone. Go back to church, keep working for the Lord, and take some time for yourself."

I was still arguing against this idea, when Everette chose the buyer for our home. Many persons wanted to buy the house, and we had over twenty contracts from which to choose. Reluctantly, I agreed to his plan. The new owner would continue to keep it as the Baldwin House for the girls. It was so hard for me to let them go. They were my life, my dream. Everette understood and tried to console me.

"Wait and see, Grace. I can almost assure you that the new owner will tire of the pace of this lifestyle. She will not be able to keep it up, and the Baldwin House will be back on the market. I predict within three years—and you can take it back if you still want it." Here Everette repeated his former advice, "Leave it alone and keep working for the Lord."

Before the final contract was signed for the sale, the mixed emotions within me had me in a turmoil that was like a smoldering fire. "This is my house. This is my life. I can't give up my dream of all the years. I can't walk out and leave all the girls." I refused to believe I could no longer handle the responsibility alone. Thinking my own determined thoughts, I paused in the dining room watching the girls enjoy their meal and fellowship together. Suddenly I announced to them, "I am not going to let anyone else have my home as Pop has planned." The anger with which I spoke was unlike the Grace the girls knew. A flash of fury had come over me like a mother hen fighting for her brood.

At that moment I leaned back against the Coke machine there in the dining room, a damp dish cloth I had been holding, still in my hand. It shocked me suddenly and threw me to the floor. There I lay, wedged behind the swinging door, unable to move and in immense pain. The girls rushed to help me up, but they were unable to budge the door. It took two ambulances to rescue me. The second one was called to bring extra equipment to remove the door so I could be lifted out. While lying there waiting I heard God speaking to me.

"Give up the house, and trust me. Follow me—not possessions and wealth—and I will show you the way. I have plans for you. Get up and spend time with your husband while he is ill."

The first ambulance took me to Johnston-Willis Hospital on Kensington Avenue. I looked up and felt Everette at my side and wondered how he could stand, knowing how weak he was. Everette had gotten out of bed when he heard all the commotion. He had wrapped a blanket around himself and insisted the other ambulance bring him to be with me.

Dr. Frank Kelly met us at the hospital and gave orders for other doctors to attend me. I had a broken collar bone, broken arm, and broken ribs. He also gave orders for nurses to take care of Everette who insisted on going into the operating room with me. They gently carried him on a stretcher to be beside me.

"What a terribly inopportune time for me to cause all this." I was crying, not only in pain. I realized that Everette had come in his grave condition because he was only thinking of me. He was spending his last days arranging everything for my future comfort. I was humbled by his unselfish concern for me. Suddenly all the anger I had felt about leaving the house, all the fiery reluctance was gone. I no longer felt ill will or resentment toward anyone. A peace "that passes all understanding" filled my heart.

After Dr. Kelly left, we learned he had stopped in to take care of us, with his usual unselfish spirit, on his way to his own son who had been injured in an automobile accident that same night. He was that kind of doctor—completely dedicated to unselfish service through all the years of his practice. Our devotion to him was the highest.

Everette and I returned home, each struggling to comfort the other one. With half of my body covered in a cast, my arm sticking out awkwardly, I never felt so low in my life. Yet all of my anger and bitterness was gone from my heart.

The next day we completed arrangements for the sale of the house. The girls were so understanding and helpful in the moving preparations.

When the time came, I was naturally sad to leave them and could not bear to say goodbye. My heart was too full, but I wanted to convey a last message of love and encouragement that would continue to be my mission. Leaving my poem on the mail table in the foyer, Everette and I closed the door behind us.

> **MOVING WITH A BROKEN ARM**
> When I arose this morning, I knelt to pray;
> I asked for guidance throughout the day.
> Then all at once, I could tell
> That everything was going well.
> For I was burdened with grief and pain,
> I thought my day's work would be in vain.
> My loved ones came and hugged me tight,
> They stayed and worked with me 'til night.
> Then grief was gone and I felt pain no more;
> I was well and happy as the day before.
> When you are weary, tired and full of grief;
> A simple prayer will restore your belief,
> And all at once you can tell
> That everything is going well.
>   - Grace R. Baldwin
>   July 11, 1973

Only a strong faith within and my deep love for my husband kept this farewell to my dream, shared with him, from being "Leaving with a Broken Heart." A quiet peace filled me as I walked away from the Baldwin House.

CHAPTER XIV

*I had fulfilled my dream before
The Baldwin House would be no more.*

"You have been a good wife to me, 'Hon." Everette looked at me as I sat at his bedside. We had been in our new home almost a year now after the first few months spent in a small apartment.

"How long have we been married—thirty-one years?" Everette was growing weaker but not in spirit. "In all those years I never caught you in but one lie."

"What? Everette! When have I ever been untruthful to you?"

"Remember when I was in the hospital, and you told me I had twenty years to live. I knew the Lord had said 'two years.' You added a zero, but that's okay. I realized why you did it." I was surprised he had known all along and had pondered it in his heart.

"Now my two years are about up." Everette continued, "I have tried to be a good husband, and I have arranged our finances so you will be comfortable even when I can't be with you. But there is something more important I want to tell you. Go back to the Baptist Church. Give your tithe, time, and talents to God. He owns all you have."

"I know. God has been so good to us." Everette and I

prayed together before calling our minister. Dr. Buddy Rosser, pastor of Monument Heights Baptist Church, was a dear friend. The beauty of that night was like a miracle as Everette expressed his faith, growing weaker with each word, but never bitter. He watched as Buddy took out his master key for the church and handed it to me.

"I know you will be a good worker at the church, Grace, and we need you there." This made Everette happy, and he smiled at me. Then Dr. Kelly came, and Everette was taken to the hospital where he died hours later on Tuesday morning. He was buried on Thursday, and I joined the church on Sunday. I found comfort and joy serving the Lord there, as Everette had known I would.

Three years later, as Everette had somehow known would happen, I received a call from the new owner of the Baldwin House. "I'm selling the Baldwin House and your mortgage."

"Oh, you can't do that!" This upset me, and I called my lawyer who assured me it was a negotiable note.

"That can be sold any time. In fact, you are in a better position now because the house still stands for the rest of your mortgage. I would advise you to take Mr. Baldwin's advice and leave that old house alone. Keep that first mortgage, and don't pick up any others until that one is paid in full."

A grandfather clause had given the Baldwin House a special permit to continue operating as a business as Pop and I had done. Now under another ownership this privilege was lost, and it was no longer to be called the Baldwin House. In time the first mortgage was paid off to me. With this next owner, debts gradually piled up against the house, necessitating, sadly, that the stately mansion be auctioned off on the City Hall steps. Again there would be new owners.

The Baldwin House had become a part of Historical Monument Avenue through the years, but the historic Baldwin House would be no more. Like the lofty statues of stone gracing the Avenue, the magnificence of the beloved "castle" would be inscribed forever in beautiful memories of all the girls, over one thousand of the very finest ladies, whose love and laughter, sunshine and music had filled

THE BALDWIN HOUSE
1953 - 1973

and fulfilled a dream. I would never forget how I had believed in that childhood dream, "Come Live With Me," and how it had come true for me. Nor would I ever forget the magic carpet from which I had first dreamed—that red velvet chair.

Come Live With Me

ALL THE GIRLS

Naomi Acree
Phyllis Alderman
Dale Alewine
Ann L. Allen
Barbara Allen
Carolyn Allen
Elaine Allen
Mary Wyllie Allen
Clara Allred
Judith Applwhite
Rickie Arendall
Betty Armstead
Jane Armstrong
Barbara Arnold
Juanita Aron
Ann Arrit
Eileen Ashberry
Martha Ashberry
Ernestine Ashburn
Barbara Ashmore
Peggy Askew
Barbara Atkins
Bernice Atkins
Hazel Atkins
Jeanette Atkins
Mildred Atkins
Paige Atkinson
Dorothy Mae Ayers
Mattie Ayers
Sharon Bailey
Bonnie Baird
Nancy O. Barden
Nancy Rose Barden
Virginia Barden
Doris Barnes
Hazel Barnett
Sylvia Barnhill
Maxine Barr
Florence Bartlett
Jo Ann Barton
Jean Baughn
Evelyn Bell
Mabel Bennett
Nancy A. Bennett
Nell Bennett
Shirley Lee Benson
Christine Berkley

Dot Bethel
Hazel Ann Bevins
Annette Bishop
Marion Bishop
Rae Bishop
Josephine Blackwell
Hilda Blankenship
Elsie Blanton
Jean Blessman
Martha Blick
Laura Blunt
Jacque Boggs
Mary Boggs
Bessie Bolock
Suzanne Booker
Helen Boster
Donna Kay Bourdon
Anne Bounds
Elaine Bowen
Sherry Bowen
June Bowles
Leslie Jean Bowles
Barbara Bowling
Anne Bowman
Cheryle Boylen
Gayle Boykin
Janie Boykin
Shirley Bradley
Jane Bragg
Barbara Brame
Linda Branch
Donna Branchin
Janice A. Brandon
Barbara Lynn Brandt
Betty Branham
Lillian Brankley
Joyce Brannon
Susie Brehm
Mildred Bresette
Nancy Breunenger
Rose Brewer
Elizabeth Broaddus
Judy Brooking
Kathleen Brookman
Kay Brooks
Grace Brothers
Barbara Brown

Jane Brown
Gloria Brown
Sharon Brown
Tina Brown
Barbara Jean Bruce
Gwen Bruce
Elnora Bryant
Lorena Bryant
Martha Bryant
Norma Bryant
Annie Gray Buchanan
Dorothy Buchanan
Lamanda Buchanan
Linda Buchanan
Shirley Buck
Linda Buckalew
Sandie Bukva
Rose Fox Bulls
Ethel Bullock
Jeane Bullock
Sarah Bullock
Janet Bunch
Virginia Burgin
Anne Price Burress
Beverly Brent Bussells
Evelyn Butler
Susan Butler
Ann Byrd
Joan Cabanis
Sharon Cain
Hilda Camden
Carol Campbell
Marion Carlton
Gladys Carpenter
Nancy Carr
Shirley Lee Carter
Joyce Casato
Sue Jo Cassell
Emily Cauthorne
Vilma Cavers
Macie Cefirs
Jane Chapman
Mary Lou Chapman
Peggy Chappbell
Page Chappell
Betty Ann Cheek
Marlene Chenault

Come Live With Me

Carolyn Childress
Lois Ann Childress
Ida Christian
Catherine Clark
Marcie Clark
Pat Clark
Paula Clark
Joyce Clary
Ruth Clawson
Anne Clay
Jayne Clement
Betty Clements
Phyllis Clevenger
Barbara Cobb
Joan Cobb
Cynthia Faye Cockrell
Penelope Cockrell
Ann Virginia Coddy
Sylvia Cogville
Joyce Sue Cohn
Barbara Coleman
Barbara Collie
Irene Eunice Collins
Kathleen Collins
Norma Jean Collins
Sue Ellen Collins
Jean Commander
Mary C. Conley
Jean Conwell
Brenda Corker
Carolyn Corley
Shirley Counts
Etta Courtney
Gwendolyn Courtney
Patricia Courtney
Alice Covington
Patricia Cowfer
Janis Cowin
Evelyn Cox
Nancy Craddock
Sandra Gayle Craig
Carol Crawford
Linda Croft
Virginia Crookshanks
Jean Cross
Dean Crowder
Elizabeth Crowder
Nancy L. Crowder
Nancy M. Crowder
Becky Crowe

Diane Crowe
Mary Crowe
Dorothy Cummins
Irma Cummins
Norma Cummins
Kathy Cupp
Carol Cushing
Jean Custalow
Anne Damerson
Charlotte Daniels
Katherine Darken
Alice Dattlegwieg
Diane Davis
Marion Davis
Joyce Davidson
Elizabeth Dawson
Nancy Dawson
Romana Dawson
Susan Dawson
Meredith Day
Judy Dayle
Margaret Deaner
Pat Dey
Mary Ann Dice
Joyce Dickerson
Kay Dickerson
Margaret Dickerson
Brenda Gale Dingus
June Dorraugh
Barbara Dorsett
Mary Dougherty
Kitty Dowdy
Myrtle Dowdy
Ora Dowdy
Mary Draper
Jane Dreury
Kay Dreury
Elizabeth Drumwright
Martha Dudley
Martha Duer
Dee Duffey
Joanne Duke
Deanna Duncan
Bambi Dunnaway
Brenda Lee Dunnaway
Betsy Dunton
Ruth A. DuPre
Ellen B. Durrette
Carol Dykes
Marjorie Ede

Diane Edwards
Faye Edwards
Frances Edwards
Annie Edgeton
Ilor Edwards
Nancy Elgin
Joyce Ellis
Carolyn Emerson
Sue Emory
Sylvia Enloe
Sandra Enlow
Ethel Epley
Fay Epps
Nancy Mae Estes
Ethel J. Everett
Katherine Eves
Joan Ewers
Robin Fail
Janie Felts
Bonnie Ferguson
Brenda Ferguson
Vaiden Ferrell
Linda Fisher
Sandy Fitchette
Barbara Fitzgerald
Gail Flippen
Adele Flora
Mary Frances Ford
Ann Foster
Bessie Foster
Lois Fowler
Charlotte France
Patricia France
Madeline Frank
Nancy Franklin
Susan Franko
Marannia Fricke
Courtney Fry
Marion Fuller
Polly Fuller
Mary A. Fulton
June Futch
Hortensia Galliano
Dottie Gardner
Betty Sue Garnett
Nonnie Garrett
Dorothy Garrison
Martha Gay
Patricia Gee
Kathy German

Come Live With Me

Donna Gholson
Dianne Gibbs
Betty Gibson
Mary Giles
Nancy Giles
Jo Ann Gill
Pat Gill
Ruby Gillespie
Pat Gilliam
Peggy Gilliand
Cathy Gilman
Joanne Gladstone
Elnora Glissom
Brenda Goft
Cynthia Goodrich
Mary Frances Goodwyn
Marjorie Gordon
Joan Helen Goss
Susan Gough
Joyce Grant
Susanne C. Grayman
Aline Green
Anne Armory Green
Loyce Green
Rita Green
Dianne Grigg
Betty Grimmell
Martha Grissom
Mary Miles Guill
Alice Gunn
Dorothy Guthrie
Emma Guthrie
Songa Hagen
Violet Hailey
Louise Haislope
Joan Hale
Constance Hall
Jean Hall
Mildred Hall
Lillian Hallandsworth
Lucy Halloway
Ottie Halterman
Margaret Hamm
Jeanette Hammer
Mary K. Hancock
Dana Hanna
Pearl Harbour
Dorothy Hardiman
Frances Hardiman
Donna Marie Harding

Rose Ann Harding
Betsy Hargrove
Ritha Harick
Betty Harmond
Minnie Harper
Sarah Harper
Sue Harper
Martha Harrell
Ann Harris
Mildred Jeanette Harris
Alice Harrup
Shirley Hart
Alice Harvey
Ann Harwell
Courtney A. Harwell
Rose H. Hawk
Ann Hawkes
Jane Hawlett
Diane Haynie
Nancy J. Haynie
Margaret J. Hedrick
Betsy Hedspeth
Carolyn Helt
Mary Alice Helwig
Sharon Henderson
Susan Henderson
Martha Hendley
Ester Hendricks
Jean Henry
Leska Hensley
Shirley Herman
Cecelia Herren
Elizabeth Herren
Missie Hersay
Mary Ann Hershbarger
Virginia Hester
Marcie Hiatt
Doris Hickman
Joan Hicks
Geraldine Hill
Jenne Hill
Lillian Hill
Patricia Hildrop
Rachel Hines
Viola Hinton
Betty K. Hitch
Carol Hogg
Marie Holc
Carol Hollowell
Rose Hollowell

Dorothy Hopkins
Gaynell Horn
Terry Howard
Betty Jane Howe
Betty L. Huber
Anne Hudgins
Dean Hudgins
Jean Hudgins
Joan Hudgins
Lillie Bell Hudgins
Linda Hudgins
Lola Hudgins
Ruby Lee Hudgins
Betty Hudson
Dean Hudson
Dottie Huffman
Louise Huger
Heather Huggins
Barbara Hughes
Rebecca Humphries
Scarlet Hunnicut
Hope Hurst
Sandra Arlene Hurst
Eric Huske
Gail Hutchins
Nancy Hyler
Sue Hylton
Theresa Hypes
Betty Ann Inge
Jennie Ingram
Suzanne Ivey
Carol Izzo
Bonnie Jackson
Linda Jamerson
Werta Jamerson
Peggy A. James
Jackie C. Jefferys
Mary Frances Jeffress
Mary D. Jeffries
Betty Jean Jenkins
Dorothy Jenkins
Grace Jenkins
Mary Sue Jenkins
Norma Jenkins
Alice Jennings
Clara Jessie
Bessie Jett
Janet Jewell
Elaine Johns
Patricia Johnson

Come Live With Me

Peggy Johnson
Anne C. Jones
Carol Jones
Jean Jones
Katie Jean Jones
Marilyn Jones
Mary Archer Jones
Patricia Jones
Patsy Jones
Theresa Jones
Catherine Jordon
Nancy Jane Journell
Ginger Jubenvill
Jane Keester
Debra Kemp
Dorothy Kennedy
Patricia Kennedy
Rebecca Kennedy
Ina Kay Kent
Rose Eileen Kientz
Carole C. King
Emily Diana King
Linda C. King
Karen E. Kinney
Evelyn E. Kish
Rosalie Kite
Helen Kody
Agnes Krakoviak
Lee Sook Kyung
Judy Labson
Christine Lambert
Wynne Lancaster
Faye Landers
Wilma Lane
Jane Langford
Laura Langford
Anne Lanier
Beverly Lapastora
Rhonda Large
Germaine Lauff
Joan Lawler
Lila Lawson
Wilma Lawson
Kitty Lea
Lauriel Hope Leary
Jane Leatherman
Donnie Lee
Margaret Leftwich
Eva Mae Leggett
Beatrice Leigh

Windfred LeSueur
Becky Lewis
Mary Lewis
Pam Linsdy
Diane Little
Lucy Little
Mary Ann Little
Genevive Lloyd
Edna Mae Lockerman
Maria Eugenia Lopez
Katherine Love
Kyle Lovett
Betty Faye Loving
Mary Ann Loving
Laura Lowery
Mary Lowman
Charlotte Ann Lumsden
Elsie Lynch
Edyth Lytton
Debra Magee
Dorothy Maham
Sandra Mahnes
Connie Maitland
Lorraine Mallet
Marie Mallet
Donnie Mann
Josephine Mann
Barbara Mantiply
Terry Markham
Lucy Ann Marshall
Rita Marshall
Sandra Marshall
Gayle Martin
Karen Martin
Junith Mason
Patricia Mason
Jean Massey
Mildred Matheny
Billie Ann McAlphin
Doris McCann
Marie Cornela McCann
Kendra McCarthy
Rebecca McCoy
Diane McCrea
Amber McCreay
Joan McCrow
Frances McDaniel
Judy McElwain
Shirley McGhee
Jane C. McKenney

Nancy McLeod
Sharon Sue McMaham
Allene McPherson
Virginia McRae
Gayle Mead
Judith Mead
Julie Medkift
Carol Meese
Patricia Mehaffie
Loretta Menchue
Joyce Messersmith
Gwendolyn Michael
Gloria Middleton
Carole Milstine
Dale Mitchel
Herakio Mitsuaha
Jean Carter Moffett
Marti Montague
Myrtle Montgomery
Mary Moody
Rose Moody
Ann Moon
Dorothy Moon
Edith Moon
Ann C. Moore
Donnie Moore
Elizabeth Moore
June Moore
Linda Moore
Nancy Conway Moore
Patricia Moore
Roberta Morand
Mary Lou Morgan
Margie Morris
Mildred Morris
Emily Morrison
Juanita Morrison
Judy Morton
Jane Moss
Phyllis Moss
Violet Moss
Mary Mothershead
Judith Mudge
Nell M. Mull
Barbara Mullins
Judy Munden
Jeannette Murfee
Judi Murphy
Patricia Murray
Louise Musser

Come Live With Me

Joan W. Myrick
Betty Jean Naff
Louise Nelson
Carolyn Newcomb
Lynn Newman
Frances Newton
Courtney Nooe
Nancy Norfleet
Edith Norman
Susan Nuckels
Betty Nunn
Mary Nunn
Muriel Nunn
Jane Nunnally
Gladys Nussil
Nancy O'Berry
Colleen O'Brien
Mickey O'Brien
Lucilly Ogelvie
Margaret Oglesby
Beverly Oleson
Elnora Oliver
Rose O'Lone
Virginia Olson
Connie Osmond
Dorothy A. Osborne
June Osmood
Barbra Owen
Elaine Owen
Jewell Owen
Ida Mae Owens
Nancy Owens
Barbara Mae Ownby
Doris Packett
Patsy Page
Cynthia Pahl
Mary K. Parrish
Thema Pavey
Ann Payne
Beatrice Payne
Lois Payntor
Betty Doug Pearce
Diane Pendergast
Alta Jane Pennington
Brenda Perry
Frances Perry
Ruby Peters
Ella H. Pfau
Amelia Phillips
Juanita Phillips

Chalie Pierce
Mary Dawn Pillow
Marie A. Pinna
Christine Pippin
Nancy Pittard
Goldie Pitts
Joyce Pitts
Theta Pitts
Martha Pomeroy
Louise Poole
Katie Poore
Gladys Portorfield
Barbara Potter
Carola Potts
Margaret Potts
Ann Powell
Barbara Powell
Faye Powell
Juanita Powell
Polly Powell
Stella Powell
Juanita Powers
Ellen Prasse
Suzie Preston
Diane Pruitt
Mary Pruitt
Mildred Puckett
Louise Puffenbarger
Barbara Puffinbargar
Betty Jean Pulley
Jean R. Race
Alpha Radford
Jane Ratcliffe
Connie Rawlings
Nellie Reams
Jane Reaves
Lois Reaves
Nancy Redvan
June Renfrow
Susan Register
Marcene Repass
Dolly Ricks
Gail Rielly
Edna Rinker
Carolyn Ripley
Anita Roak
Mary Ann Roane
Rue Roberts
Terry Robertson
Dorothy Robinson

Cindy Robison
Doris Ann Rock
Tencha Rodeagur
Iris Rodreguez
Carolyn Rogers
Imogene Rogerson
Nell Roper
Partlow Roper
Virginia Roper
Addie Rosen
Peggy Rosser
Jean Rowe
Myrtle Rowe
Linda Royster
Juanita Rumberg
Linda Rush
Doris Russell
Gladys Russell
Kitty Russell
Nancy Ryder
Catherine Ryland
Anita Sadler
Glena Sands
Mildred Sangster
Louise Saterfield
Alline Saunders
Mary Saver
Arrienia Sayler
Nancy Saylor
Lou Ann Schench
Barbara Schenkle
Shirley Schmidt
Susan Scruggs
Frances Seay
Jean Seay
Betty Sedwick
Eva Marie Selagiewicz
Sheryl Semprevivo
Linda Shackelford
Beatrice Shackleford
Gail Shaft
Gladys Sharp
Delilah Shaver
Jo Ann Sheets
Gaynell Shelton
Betty Joe Sheviely
Judi Shuler
Allyne Shutters
Jean Shields
Billie Jean Shores

Come Live With Me

Roberta Shores
Shirley Shores
Barbara Simmons
Ella Ann Simmons
Jane Simmons
Judy Simmons
Lois Simms
Alice Simoneau
Meta Simpson
Mary Singleton
Dorothy Sinlock
Lola Sisk
Kimberly Sissons
Myrt Sivley
Linda Slate
Carole Sluder
Amelda Smith
Kathleen Smith
Lori Smith
Louise Smith
Montrose Smith
Nancy Lea Smith
Roberta Smith
Sarah Ann Smith
Virginia R. Smith
Nancy Snoddy
Janice South
Kay Southerland
Linda Southerland
Madelyn Spade
Nancy Sparks
Martha Spence
Nancy Spencer
Sallie Spencer
Flossie Spicer
Betty Ann Sprouse
Shirley Sprouse
Tiffany Sprouse
Virginia Sprouse
Grace Stainback
Janice Stauffer
Joyce Stankiel
Arline Stanley
Margie Stanley
Phyllis Stanley
Mary Stanton
Shirley Stanton
Cleo Starks
Joanna Stubbs
Brenda Swann

Diane Swann
Louise Swartz
Frances Stegall
Doris Stephens
Rue Stephens
Sue Stephenson
Vonnie Stiefuater
Joyce Still
Gloria Stolz
Betty Jean Stone
Tammy Street
Ann Sugg
Lila Sutphin
Paulette E. Taft
Nancy Talbott
Helen Tatterson
Adele Taylor
Clara A. Taylor
Doris Marie Taylor
Jean Taylor
Lillian Taylor
Mary Lynn Taylor
Phyllis Tellis
Helen Thacker
Jean Thaxton
Dianne Thomas
Connie Thompson
Jane Thrift
Sallie Thrift
Mary Ann Thrope
Winona M. Thrope
Suzanne Tignor
Ruth Timmons
Pamela Timms
Jean Tinsley
Judy Tinsley
Freda Toler
Judi Anne Tolson
Joan Tomes
Virginia Tomlinson
Audrey Toms
Sue Topping
Barbara Townsend
Jean Trader
Patricia Trader
Alice Traenham
Jane Trump
Patricia Traylor
Kitt Tucker
Andy Turlington

Eva Nell Turner
Susan Turner
Ellen Tyler
Linda Underwood
Carole Ann Utley
Delores Vaughan
Patricia Vest
Peggy Sue Via
Shirley Vipperman
Patricia Waddel
Sue Wadford
Kitty Wagner
Ann Walker
Jewell Wall
Dorothy Walsh
Christine Walton
Marianne Ward
Edith Earl Warren
Shelby Washburn
Doris Waxmunski
Elsie Wayne
Juanita Weeks
Ruth Wells
Lois West
Peggy Anne Westbrook
Ann Wester
Julie Wheay
Pauline Whelchel
Shirley Whisenhunt
Elizabeth Whitby
Diane White
Joyce Christine White
Winfred White
Dorothy Whitehead
Pam Whitley
Helen Whitlock
Alice Ann Whitmore
Susan Whittazer
Linda Wickland
Jackie Wilder
Evelyn Wilkerson
Judy Wilkerson
Katheryn Wilkerson
Ricki Lou Wilkerson
Mary Lou Wilkes
Audrey Wilkins
Charlotte Willbourne
AnneWilliams
Barbara Kay Williams
Bernice Williams

Come Live With Me

Bessie Jean Williams	Jean Winner	Monica Wright
Jeannie Williams	Joyce Wirtz	Nancy Wright
Jill Williams	Mildred Wiseman	Kim Wyatt
June Williams	Gwen Withers	Victoria Wyatt
Maryann Williams	Jean Wolf	Betsy Young
Patricia Williams	Patricia Wood	Elaine Young
Sue Ann Williams	Shirley Wood	Etta Young
Susan P. Williams	Barbara Woodfin	Mary Ann Young
Clayshia Wills	Alice Barnes Woodruft	Mary Lou Young
Priscilla Wilmoth	Uldine Woodruft	Jackie Ann Younger
Alice Wilson	Anne Woods	Lavome Younger
Carole Wilson	Mary Jane Woodson	Katherine Yuome
Kay Wilson	Joan Lee Wright	Rosina A. Zangari
Louise Wilson	Linda Wright	
Sue Wilson	Margaret Wright	

Although this list is long and may be incomplete, I wish to thank all the girls, their boyfriends and husbands, and the students of law, dentistry and pharmacy that filled our home with love and respect. I dedicate this book with pride to those to whom Pop and I said, "Come live with us." I offer my special thanks to God always, and to all the dear people who said, "Come live with me," and made my life so full of golden memories.